# SAMUEL MARSDEN

PREACHER, PASTOR, MAGISTRATE AND MISSIONARY

## DAVID B. PETTETT

*Samuel Marsden.*
*Preacher, Pastor, Magistrate and Missionary*
Studies in Australian Colonial History (ISSN 1834-6936) No. 5
© David B. Pettett 2016

Bolt Publishing Services Pty. Ltd.
ABN 89 123 024 920
PO Box 147
Camperdown NSW 1450
www.boltpublishing.com.au

**National Library of Australia Cataloguing-in-Publication entry (pbk)**

| | |
|---|---|
| **Creator:** | Pettett, David B., author. |
| **Title:** | Samuel Marsden : preacher, pastor, magistrate and missionary / David B. Pettett. |
| **ISBN:** | 9780994634900 (paperback) |
| **Series:** | Studies in Australian colonial history; 5, |
| **Notes:** | Includes bibliographical references. |
| **Subjects:** | Marsden, Samuel, 1765-1838. |
| | Church of England—Clergy—Biography. |
| | Clergy—New South Wales—Biography. |
| | Police magistrates—New South Wales—Biography. |
| | Missionaries—New Zealand—Biography. |
| | Missionaries—Tahiti—Biography. |
| | Australia—History—1788-1900. |
| **Dewey Number:** | 266.0092 |

Cover design and layout by Lankshear Design.
Printed by Ingram Spark Lightning Source.

# PUBLISHER'S PREFACE

MANY OF THE UNTOLD stories in Australian Colonial History belong to Christian people who, with all their strengths and weaknesses, contributed greatly to the building of Australian Society. Before readily available and multiform media, the regular weekly sermon preached on Sundays and at weekly prayer meetings was an important part of the living communication that regularly shaped such people.

Although the number of sermons preached in the English penal colony of New South Wales can be estimated to be in the hundreds of thousands, historians of the Australian Colonial period are only just beginning to explore the value of these sermons for understanding some of the social realities of our past.[1]

In this context, David Pettett provides a new and welcome contribution to understanding Rev Samuel Marsden, a colourful figure already of interest to Australian historians, under the illumination provided by Marsden's surviving sermons. Well aware of Marsden's human faults, this brief account corrects previous errors, and shows a man dedicated to the service of Jesus Christ for the benefit of early Australasia.

Peter G. Bolt                                                        August 2016

---

[1] See M. Gladwin, 'Preaching and Australian public life: 1788–1914', *Preaching Before a Watching World, St Mark's Review*, 227 (Feb, 2014), 1–14 (especially pp.2-3, 10); and the collection of articles published in *Preaching and Sermons in Australian History Since 1788, St Mark's Review*, 230 (Dec, 2014).

## STUDIES IN AUSTRALIAN COLONIAL HISTORY
ISSN 1834-6936

1. Peter G. Bolt, *Thomas Moore of Liverpool (1762–1840): One of Our Oldest Colonists. Essays & Addresses to Celebrate 150 Years of Moore College* (2007).

2. Peter G. Bolt, *William Cowper (1778–1858). The Indispensable Parson. The Life and Influence of Australia's First Parish Clergyman* (2009).
   a. Full-text Edition
   b. Commemorative Pictorial Edition produced for Cowper200.

3. Peter G. Bolt, *A Portrait in his Actions. Thomas Moore of Liverpool (1762–1840). Part 1: Lesbury to Liverpool* (2010)

4. Peter G. Bolt, *A Portrait in his Actions. Thomas Moore of Liverpool (1762–1840). Part 2: Liverpool to Legacy* (forthcoming)

5. David B. Pettett, *Samuel Marsden. Preacher, Pastor, Magistrate and Missionary* (2016)

6. Peter G. Bolt (Ed.), *Freedom to Libel? Samuel Marsden v Philo Free: Australia's First Libel Case* (2016)

7. David B. Pettett, *The Sermons Of Samuel Marsden. A Critical Edition* (forthcoming).

DAVID PETTETT's treatment of Marsden shows us what was at the heart of his preaching. The focus on Samuel Marsden as an evangelical preacher in the early colony helps to redress some of the negativity about the man by revealing his theological and pastoral concern for those he addressed. Everyone interested in the influence of evangelicalism in the early colony will benefit from reading this account.

*Colin Bale,*
*Vice Principal Moore College*

UNTIL NOW BIOGRAPHERS of Samuel Marsden have ignored the main source of evidence about him – his sermons. David Pettett has made a close study of all his sermons and transcribed them for the benefit of us all. In this valuable and concise account surprising new light is thrown on the most controversial of Christ's ambassadors in Australian history. Marsden will continue to have his critics, but now his own motivation will be better understood, his pastor's heart for his people appreciated, and his strategic approach to mission admired. How David Pettett uses the sermons will also be admired, especially his reconstruction of his most famous sermon, that which he preached at the Bay of Islands on Christmas Day 1814.

*Associate Professor Stuart Piggin,*
*Assoc Prof – Ancient History. Macquarie University*

THOUGH A MUCH-MALIGNED figure in Australian history, Samuel Marsden had at least been seen more positively in New Zealand. But, as this engaging short study shows, Marsden was the same man, driven by the gospel imperative to attempt much, which he did with all his might but with inevitable human flaws and weaknesses. Particularly marked in David Pettett's approach is his meticulous research, courageous tackling of very contentious issues, the careful contextualization of his subject and his balanced judgements. His deep knowledge of, and careful analysis of Marsden's sermons give great richness to his recreation of Marsden's spiritual and moral universe.

Professor Malcolm Prentis,<br>Honorary Professor of Australian Catholic University

I'M GRATEFUL TO DAVID PETTETT for his deep insight into Marsden, as a man, a passionate missionary and a controversial magistrate in his own times, times that were vastly different to our own. Every insight is built on the original documents and especially Marsden's sermons. This is a beautifully balanced account of Marsden, his faults and his great achievements.

Rev. Canon Bruce Morrison,<br>Rector St. John's Anglican Regional Cathedral Parramatta

# CONTENTS

**INTRODUCTION** . . . . . . . . . . . . . . . . . . . . . . . . . . . . . . . . . . . . . . . . . . . . 9

**CHAPTER ONE** Marsden's Ministry . . . . . . . . . . . . . . . . . . . . . . . . . 13
    Influence of Charles Simeon . . . . . . . . . . . . . . . . . . . . . . . . . . 17

**CHAPTER TWO** The Magistrate . . . . . . . . . . . . . . . . . . . . . . . . . . . . 19

**CHAPTER THREE** The New Zealand Mission . . . . . . . . . . . . . . . . . 22
    Great Commission . . . . . . . . . . . . . . . . . . . . . . . . . . . . . . . . . 23
    Strategic Thinker . . . . . . . . . . . . . . . . . . . . . . . . . . . . . . . . . . 25
    Sanction and Strategy . . . . . . . . . . . . . . . . . . . . . . . . . . . . . . 29
    One great work of God . . . . . . . . . . . . . . . . . . . . . . . . . . . . . 30
    Criticisms of Wealth . . . . . . . . . . . . . . . . . . . . . . . . . . . . . . . 32
    The Mission Delayed . . . . . . . . . . . . . . . . . . . . . . . . . . . . . . 34
    Ruatara . . . . . . . . . . . . . . . . . . . . . . . . . . . . . . . . . . . . . . . . . 38
    Finally Underway . . . . . . . . . . . . . . . . . . . . . . . . . . . . . . . . . 40
    The Sermon . . . . . . . . . . . . . . . . . . . . . . . . . . . . . . . . . . . . . 48

**CHAPTER FOUR** Marsden and Macquarie . . . . . . . . . . . . . . . . . . . 50
    A difficult relationship – the Beginnings . . . . . . . . . . . . . . . 52
    Death of Ellis Bent . . . . . . . . . . . . . . . . . . . . . . . . . . . . . . . . 58
    A Public Dressing Down . . . . . . . . . . . . . . . . . . . . . . . . . . . 60

The Sins of the People ... 61
The real thrust ... 63
The Significance of the Death of Ellis Bent ... 66
Marsden and Authority ... 69

**CHAPTER FIVE** The Preacher and his People ... 71
The Exclusives ... 76
The Gallows, Innocent Men and Women of Shame ... 80
Marriage and Adultery ... 84
On Magistrates and the rule of law ... 90
The Natives of this Colony ... 93
Prostitution, Sobriety and Children ... 98
Sabbath neglect, Gambling and other sins ... 105
The general character of the people of the colony ... 109
On sodomy ... 110
On reviling ... 112
On extortion and avarice ... 113
Covetousness ... 116
On the receiving of stolen goods ... 117
On foul language ... 118
Soil Notes ... 119
Christian Charity ... 122

**CONCLUSION** ... 123

**SELECT BIBLIOGRAPHY** ... 127

# INTRODUCTION

THE REV SAMUEL MARSDEN was the second chaplain to the colony of New South Wales and the first minister of the parish church of St. John's Parramatta. He served there from when he first arrived in the colony in 1794 until his death in 1838. While he held this position he also became a successful and wealthy farmer. Before the more famous John McArthur reached his stride, Marsden exported Australia's first fine wool clip. He established the first Christian mission to New Zealand where, today, he is still known as the Apostle to the Māori. He also became a magistrate in the colony, earning himself the title of Flogging Parson. Marsden was, and remains, a controversial figure. For more than 200 years he has had his supporters and detractors.

The Australian historian Robert Hughes describes Marsden as, "a grasping Evangelical missionary with heavy shoulders and the face of a petulant ox". He declares that Marsden's "hatred for the Irish Catholic convicts knew no bounds. It spilled into his sermons".[1] However, a close examination of all the extant copies of Marsden's sermons reveals that he makes no reference at all to the Irish or to Catholics in any sermon.

---

1   Robert Hughes. *The Fatal Shore: A History of Transportation of Convicts to Australia, 1787–1868*. London, The Havill Press. 1987. p. 187.

Marsden's original sermons sit in various collections around the world but historians have not made much use of them. My own research has been on those sermons and it has been a surprise to see some new light being shed on some of the controversial issues he faced, as for example these comments by Hughes.

Marsden described himself as first and foremost a preacher. In one of his sermons he says that the primary role of the office of a minister is "to preach the gospel of Christ". With this self-understanding, any study of Marsden that seeks to understand his personality and motivations must include study of his sermons. Without reference to his sermons any conclusions must inevitably be tentative.

In various collections around the world there are 135 sermons, some of which are fragments. Moore Theological College Library in Sydney holds 98. There are 25 in the Family Collection and the remainder are scattered in ones and twos in various libraries and archives in Australia and New Zealand.

Hughes and other critics are not the only ones who have made mistakes about Marsden because they have not referred to his sermons. Even Marsden's supporters have made mistakes and misunderstood his motivations and the influences on him because they have not studied his preaching.[2]

From his role as a harsh magistrate in a penal colony to a pastor caring for his people, the following chapters delve into Marsden's sermons to bring new understanding of his complex character.

---

2   For an excellent and full biography of Marsden see A. T. Yarwood, *Samuel Marsden: The Great Survivor*. Carlton, Vic. Melbourne University Press. 1977. Yarwood does, however, make some mistakes particularly misunderstanding that the major influence on Marsden's preaching came from his Cambridge mentor, the Rev Charles Simeon.

The sermons throw light on what Marsden thought he was doing in leading a mission to New Zealand, highlighting his attitudes to the "native people" of both Australia and New Zealand. He was criticised for neglecting ministry to the Aboriginal people while focusing on the Māori. He was also criticised for neglecting "the duties of his parish" while he engaged in trade in the South Seas. His sermons show, for the first time, Marsden's own thinking on these issues.

Marsden's relationship with perhaps the most significant of the colonial governors, Lachlan Macquarie, was not an easy one. Macquarie arrived in the colony in 1810 and found himself almost in immediate conflict with the chaplain. In 1815 Macquarie gave Marsden a public dressing down following a sermon he took particular exception to. Macquarie finally broke off relations completely with Marsden at the beginning of 1818. The sermon which earned Marsden the governor's ire in 1815 is dealt with in Chapter Four. It highlights a number of issues about Marsden's character and reputation, giving some insight not previously understood by historians and other Marsden commentators.

This book is written primarily with the congregation of St John's Parramatta, and those who visit this historic building, in mind. It is hoped that those who gather and those who visit this landmark of Sydney's colonial era, will gain some sense of Marsden, the preacher of the "everlasting gospel", as they hear Marsden's words in the quotations that follow and see in their mind's eye the pastor with his people in the place he spent his entire ministry.[3]

---

3   For Marsden's sermons, see D.B. Pettett, *The Sermons of Samuel Marsden. A Critical Edition* (forthcoming).

## CHAPTER ONE
# MARSDEN'S MINISTRY

Samuel Marsden arrived in the colony of New South Wales in March 1794 and began ministry at Parramatta soon after. Essentially, he spent his entire ministry there, becoming senior Chaplain to the colony after the first chaplain, Richard Johnson who had come on the First Fleet in 1788, returned to England in 1800.

Marsden has an enduring legacy. He is still known today in New South Wales as the "Flogging Parson" yet in New Zealand he is the "Apostle to the Māori". That a man could, in general terms, be despised by many in New South Wales and yet loved by most in New Zealand, gives rise to questions, interest and speculation that Marsden was no ordinary man.

The opinions which have coloured his reputation now for over two hundred years are not to be taken at face value as self-evident truths. The extremes of these opinions alert us to the fact that here is a man of deep complexity who cannot be so easily categorized, whether he be demonized by his enemies or sanctified by his friends. We must also keep in mind what Marsden said about himself. What did he think he was doing as he set out to become the second chaplain to the colony? What were his dispositions toward convicts, his flock, and key historical figures? Why did he take to New Zealand? Much light is shed on these types of questions by Marsden's sermons.

Marsden was born at Farsley, U.K. on 26 June, 1765. He was the oldest of seven children by his father, Thomas, a butcher, and in his teens was apprenticed to his uncle to learn the art of blacksmithing. In October, 1786 Marsden began his formal education in the home of the Rev Samuel Stones, a member of the Elland Clerical Society, who, as tradition has it, first met Marsden when he brought his horse to be shod at his uncle's foundry. In 1788 Marsden moved to Hull to further his education under the Rev Joseph Milner. From Hull he entered Magdalene College Cambridge on 7 December, 1790. After just two years and before he had completed his degree, the Rev Charles Simeon recommended Marsden for the chaplaincy at Botany Bay. Before leaving for this assignment Marsden married Elizabeth Fristan. The Marsdens' first child, Ann, was born on the ship just a few days before arriving in Port Jackson, NSW on 10 March, 1794.

While on board ship ready to set out to the colony in 1793 Marsden remarked in his journal that he was about to quit his homeland in order to preach the everlasting gospel. He expressed the desire that, "the end of my going may be answered in the Conversion of many poor Souls".[4]

Marsden was an evangelical churchman at heart, a product of the evangelical milieu. Evangelicalism not only shaped his character and the decisions he made in ministry. Marsden took a deep and personal interest in the evangelical movement around the world. In particular his interest in, support of, and involvement with the

---

4   Samuel Marsden, *Diary – 1793–1794*. Mitchell Library, C245. Entry dated 27 July, 1793.

Baptist Missionary Society, the London Missionary Society and the Church Missionary Society is evidenced not only by his personal involvement with the latter two but also in his own preaching. His sermons show he was focused on the progress of the gospel which at times left him blinkered to the impressions others were developing about his ministry and the motives they were imputing to him.

After arriving in the colony, Marsden quickly came into conflict with Lieutenant Governor Grose over the issue of convicts attending church on Sundays. A year later when Hunter became governor life for Marsden became a little easier. Hunter had trained for ministry in the Presbyterian Church. He appointed Johnson and Marsden as civil magistrates in which position Marsden served until he returned to England in 1807.

In 1798 Marsden welcomed missionaries of the London Missionary Society fleeing Tahiti and was officially appointed as resident agent and supervisor of the Society's operations in the South Seas in 1804. Despite warnings from home that he should not associate with the dissenters, Marsden saw in his fellow evangelicals the opportunities for gospel ministry. Marsden's reputation, power and influence increased during the governorship of King (1800–1806). According to the colonial botanist George Caley, Marsden effectively became second-in-command in the affairs of the colony during this time.

In 1807 Marsden left the colony to recruit teachers, chaplains and missionaries from the United Kingdom. He returned to New South Wales with some success in February, 1810. On this trip he secured from the Church Missionary Society missionaries to accompany him back to New South Wales to begin a mission to New Zealand. Delays to this mission saw Marsden writing to the CMS asking that the missionaries be put to work in the colony until such time that they might be able to continue their journey on to New Zealand. It would be another four years before Marsden and the CMS missionaries could begin that mission.

During his absence from the colony Marsden avoided the difficulties during the governorship of Bligh and the subsequent rebellion. Bligh became governor in August 1806. After antagonising many merchants and military men in the colony he was finally arrested in January 1808. In March 1809 he sailed to Hobart, returning to Sydney in January 1810 after Lachlan Macquarie had been appointed as his replacement. Marsden returned in February to discover that Macquarie was now Governor. The conflict between these two men is the focus of special attention in Chapter Four.

Marsden began his mission to New Zealand in December 1814. He preached the first Christian sermon in New Zealand on Christmas Day that year. In all, he was to make a total of seven journeys to New Zealand to advance the mission. The last of these was in 1837, less than a year before his death.

Having produced eight children, five girls and three boys, two of whom died in infancy in tragic circumstances, Marsden's beloved "Betsy", who had suffered a debilitating stroke in 1811, died in October, 1835. Marsden himself died in the Rectory at Windsor on 12 May, 1838.

Through his long ministry in the colony the society to which Marsden came and preached went through significant changes. His sermons show that on occasion Marsden was addressing convicts. He was never a man to mince his words. "Many of you", he said in one sermon, "have formed unlawful communions with the most abandoned of the human race. For these you toil and sweat. For these you rob and plunder …" (Sermon 7:23). On other occasions a more genteel audience is evident.

## Influence of Charles Simeon

Amongst his many friends and mentors the influence of the Rev Charles Simeon, fellow of King's College and Vicar of Holy Trinity Church, Cambridge, upon Marsden is second to none and cannot be overestimated. This influence shaped Marsden's character as an evangelical and formed him to be entirely dependent on Simeon's preaching style. Simeon published over 3,000 sermon outlines in 21 volumes. Marsden used these extensively. This dependence led to a major criticism. Marsden was said to have put very little of his own work into his sermons but simply dished up Simeon's outlines. This criticism added weight to the controversy that Marsden spent little time working as a chaplain but was more interested in temporal affairs than his ministry.

A comparison of Marsden's sermons with Simeon's outlines shows that he was in fact slavishly dependent on the outlines. Yet a close study of the sermons also shows that Marsden put a lot of his own work into them. While in his sermons Marsden was direct, blunt and even harsh at times, the typical phrasing of his words shows that he had a pastoral concern for the people he was speaking to. He did not harangue them, but used inclusive language. The preacher identified with his people and spoke in the first person plural. In Sermon 10:15[5], for example he does not rebuke his congregation for *their* behaviour but he speaks of "*our* wicked works". He put a lot of work into the preparation of his

---

5   Most references to sermons throughout this book are by number as they appear in the Moore Theological College Library catalogue, the largest collection of Marsden's sermons. References to pages in the sermons are by the number of the sermon followed by a colon and the page number, so that Sermon Ten and Page Fifteen, for example, is rendered as 10:15. Where reference is made to a sermon in another collection that collection is identified.

sermons so that he was speaking as a pastor to his people in their context.

## CHAPTER TWO

# THE MAGISTRATE

It may come as a surprise to modern readers that Marsden became a magistrate. While this was not a common occurrence of the time, it was not unusual in rural England. Often the local parson was the only educated man available to administer the law. In the early days of colonial Australia this was even more the case. Parsons, doctors, merchants and ship builders were given the responsibility of administering the law in New South Wales. None of them had any training to do this.

Thomas Moore, the former ship builder who settled with his emancipated wife in Liverpool, New South Wales, was one person appointed as a magistrate with no experience. He was on the bench in Liverpool. In the early 1820s Governor Brisbane instituted an enquiry into how justice was being served in the colony. The results were tabled in the House of Commons in 1826. Moore was named in this submission as being one of several magistrates in New South Wales who had ordered illegal punishment to gain information about a crime.

The magistrates were often faced with accused men refusing to give information to the court. It was not uncommon for the bench to issue an order that the unfortunate soul should be flogged until he gave up the information. This type of torture being administered by the judiciary in the colony seems to have become something of the norm. The members of the Commons were not so much interested in the severity of punishments in New South Wales, but in their legality. In legal action that followed this inquiry Moore pleaded ignorance saying, we "had not much reference to law in those times".[6]

Marsden is known to have been involved in these illegal punishments. And yet his reputation as the Flogging Parson seems to have come more from the severity of his punishments. He believed that his reputation as a harsh magistrate first arose from criticism by Governor Macquarie in 1817. Marsden defended himself against these accusations declaring that the Governor had set limits on the punishments magistrates could impose and that he had never exceeded these. He also argued that as the magistrate in the most notorious district of the colony, namely Parramatta, it should be no surprise that he handed down more punishments than any other magistrate.

Yet Macquarie was not the only person to accuse Marsden of being a harsh magistrate. An enquiry into the state of the colony and the effectiveness of transportation in deterring crime in the U.K. was decided upon by Lord Bathurst in 1817. John Thomas Bigge arrived in Port Jackson 26 September, 1819 to conduct the enquiry. In his report Bigge declared that Marsden's "sentences are not only, in fact, more severe than those of the other magistrates, but that the general opinion of the colony is, that his character, as displayed in the administration of the penal law in New South Wales, is stamped with severity". Bigge, however, tempered his estimation

---

6   *Sydney Gazette* 20 December, 1826.

of Marsden by saying this assessment was made, "without stating it as my opinion that he has acted with undue severity", and that, "I am far from entertaining an opinion that it forms part of Mr. Marsden's natural character".

## CHAPTER THREE
# THE NEW ZEALAND MISSION

AMONGST HIS MANY activities and responsibilities Marsden thought that the mission to New Zealand was his most important work.

On the beach at Rangihoua in the north of the Bay of Islands, New Zealand, Marsden preached what is regarded as the first Christian sermon in New Zealand on Christmas Day, 1814. Contemporaries and later historians have criticised him for this mission, believing that by engaging in it he was at once neglecting the Australian Aboriginal and seeking to gain for himself both wealth and reputation. Certainly, Marsden expressed that his focus was fully on the mission to New Zealand despite other matters of a pressing private and public nature. To Josiah Pratt, secretary of the CMS, he wrote of the New Zealand mission, "this I consider of more importance than any other, and feel it my call to follow the openings of Providence".

The conduct of the mission certainly shows Marsden's strength of character in the face of controversial assessments by others. From his many years of strategic planning, negotiating and equipping, to the fulfilment of the establishment of the CMS mission to New Zealand we see Marsden as a man of vision who persevered in the face of many setbacks to achieve what he had long believed was the calling of a benevolent God.

## Great Commission

Marsden viewed the Great Commission of Matthew 28:19, "make disciples of all nations", as encompassing a promise. He believed that until the gospel had been preached to all nations, "this commission will not be fully executed". Marsden believed that the promise encompassed in the words of the Great Commission was that God, "would save the heathens, and take out of them a people for himself". He believed that:

> These words ... give the missionaries of the gospel of peace a roving commission. They have authority from the King of Kings to navigate all seas, to visit every island upon the bosom of the great deep, to traverse all continents, to sound the silver trumpet of jubilee, and to inform the nations of the earth that the year of release is at hand, and to invite the ransomed sinners to return to their once forfeighted (sic) possessions. God had promised by the mouth of all his prophets that he would save the heathens, and take out of them a people for himself. (Sermon 34:2)

What's more, Marsden believed this "roving commission" applied to himself. Leaving his homeland for the first time in 1793 Marsden's desire was to see "the Conversion of many poor Souls". He was going to the South Seas "to preach the everlasting gospel".

His sponsors hoped that the Rev Richard Johnson, who had arrived at Botany Bay in the First Fleet in 1788 as the first chaplain to New South Wales, would be gracious enough to share with Marsden the title of "Apostle to the South Seas".[7] Government authorities thought they were getting a chaplain simply to engender a sense of morality in the convicts and soldiers. But with expectations of seeing the gospel proclaimed throughout the South Seas, Johnson and Marsden had other ideas. Marsden in particular was not about to dish up a "scanty morality". His purpose was "to publish the glad tidings of a free and full salvation to a lost world".

At a very early stage, the evangelical leaders of the Church of England were active in efforts to see the evangelical gospel proclaimed throughout the British Empire and beyond. Wilberforce, through his friendship with Pitt, made sure that the First Fleet sailed to Botany Bay with a chaplain. Simeon had developed a close relationship with Charles Grant of the East India Company and was actively recommending young evangelical preachers to him as chaplains. It is no surprise therefore that these two men, Wilberforce and Simeon, along with the Rev John Venn and others, were key in the establishment of the Church Missionary Society in 1799. It was to this Society that Marsden suggested in April 1808 that the people of New Zealand were a "very superior people in point of mental endowments" and therefore provided a fertile ground for the bringing of civilisation and the gospel. It was Marsden's idea that the Society should provide the fruits of civilisation by sending artisan missionaries who would simultaneously bring the arts of civilisation and the proclamation of the gospel. Those who believe Marsden emphasised the fruits of civilisation as a necessary

---

[7] John Newton, Letter to the Rev Richard Johnson 24 May 1793. HRNSW Vol. 2. p. 27.

precursor to the bringing of the gospel have misunderstood Marsden's careful, nuanced and strategic thinking about mission.

On the contrary, Marsden expected that his missionaries would take the arts of civilisation as well as the proclamation of the everlasting gospel. To the Church Missionary Society, he said, "Though the Missionaries might employ a certain portion of their time, according to local circumstances, in manual labour, this neither would nor ought to prevent them from constantly endeavouring to instruct the natives in the great doctrines of the Gospel". Indeed, as Marsden took the first missionaries to New Zealand in 1814 he began the Mission with a very clear and detailed proclamation of the "Glad tidings of great joy" from Luke 2:10. At a much earlier time, once he had reflected on the failure of the first missionary efforts to Tahiti, Marsden wrote to the Directors of the London Missionary Society about "the absurdity of the idea of the missionaries employing their time only in conversing and instructing the natives". In this letter Marsden's idea was that it was absurd to expect missionaries to do nothing but preach. Yet his priority was not "civilisation first", but rather "gospel and civilisation together".[8]

## Strategic Thinker

On his return journey to New South Wales on board the *Ann* in 1809 Marsden took the opportunity to learn the Māori language as he met up again with the young Māori Chief, Ruatara, whom he had probably first met back in the colony in September 1806. This

---

8   Marsden to LMS Directors, 30 Jan 1801

is indicative of his purpose, foresight and long term planning to take the gospel to the New Zealanders in their own language.

Equally instructive of his strategic missionary thinking is Sermon 34 in the Moore Theological College Collection. In this sermon Marsden speaks of the work of various British missionary societies around the world. The sermon shows that Marsden was not just pleased to see the gospel being proclaimed around the world but that he believed that the places where the gospel was sounding forth had been chosen for their strategic locations. For example when speaking about the establishment of missionary work by the Church Missionary Society in western Africa in Sermon 34:12-15 Marsden says,

> If the Christian religion once begins to send forth its living waters on the shores of western (Africa), it will soon spread its fertilizing streams thru its burning deserts, and turn that barren wilderness into a fruitful field. The voice of joy and gladness will be heard in those dreary regions of moral darkness, where the poor ignorant African pays his devotions to demons.

Marsden clearly believed the effect of this proclamation begun on the west coast would be the conversion of the African continent:

> The same almighty word which said, let there be light and there was light, can command the Son of Righteousness to arise upon Africa with healing under his wings. Africa shall then (be free, shall then) be enlightened with divine truth, the glory of the Lord shall be revealed amongst them, and the kingdom of Satan shall fall like lightning from heaven, and they shall hear no more the voice of the oppressor. ... The only object of the society in their benevolent exertions

here, is to free Africa from the bondage of sin and Satan, from the oppressions and cruelties of the slave trade and from the intestine *(sic: internecine)* wars connected with that bloody traffic.

Marsden's vision for Africa was large. He has recounted in the sermon the deeds of the missionaries and the difficulties they had faced; how settlements and schools had been burned; how, "When one missionary has fallen a sacrifice to the climate, another hath stept *(sic)* into his station and filled up the broken rank". He records successes where "Two churches have been erected, and schools opened for more than 2000 native children many of whom have been redeemed from slavery". And yet as exciting and as hopeful as these missionary efforts were, Marsden's vision was raised to see beyond this western coastal fringe to see the whole continent being won for Christ. As he continued in the sermon to speak about the work of the CMS in Malta, again he believed it was a strategic decision to have begun the work there. He speaks of Malta as a central location for the spread of the gospel throughout the Greek islands and also onto the African continent where it was his hope that the gospel would, "in due time spread its branches over Egypt, and the various nations in that part of the globe". He says "The seed which the society is now scattering in the Mediterranean tho at present as small as a grain of mustard seed may grow into a great tree" (Sermon 34:16). In this sermon as Marsden recounted the efforts of missionaries in Africa and the Mediterranean, he also looked beyond those particular efforts, with a strategic focus, to see greater things being accomplished through these small beginnings. Similarly, this was his hope for the mission to New Zealand.

Marsden's vision was not limited to what the Societies were doing in Africa, the Mediterranean and North America. Nor was it limited to what he was doing in New South Wales and New Zealand. As he had brought with him the expectation of John Newton that he and Richard Johnson would share the title "Apostle to the South Seas", Marsden believed that the establishment of a British colony in New South Wales was a providential ordering for the spread of the gospel throughout the South Seas. He expressed the thought as early as 1812 that:

> The Colony promises to become a place of great importance to all the South Sea Islands. It is from N S Wales that proper missionaries are to be raised up for the instruction of the heathen in these parts. I trust that some of the rising generation will become a seed to sow the land.

His wish that "some of the rising generation" would become those missionaries to the South Seas was fulfilled in what may be a most unexpected way. A man who was a single missionary from Tahiti had fallen in love with the daughter of former convicts who had since become "pious". Malcolm Falloon comments:

> In a sense, this was Marsden's emancipationist agenda for the Colony – that, unlike North America, God would evangelize the South Sea Islands, not using, said Marsden, "an army of pious Christians" or "men of character and of principle", but men taken, "from the dregs of society – the sweepings of the gaols, hulks, and prisons".[9]

---

9   Malcolm Falloon, '"Openings of Providence": The shaping of Marsden's missionary vision for New Zealand.' In Peter G. Bolt & David B. Pettett Eds. *Launching Marsden's Mission; The Beginnings of the Church Missionary Society in New Zealand, viewed from New South Wales.* London. Latimer Press. 2014. p. 133. Falloon quotes from Marsden, in *Missionary Register* (1823), p.66.

## Sanction and Strategy

Marsden came under heavy sanction from various quarters when he launched his mission to New Zealand. The declaration by Secretary Campbell in his libellous *Philo Free* letter in the *Sydney Gazette* that Marsden's voyage to New Zealand to establish the mission demonstrated a supposed lack of interest in the Aboriginal people of New South Wales was not just disingenuous but an error of fact.

Like Johnson before him, who had brought a young Aboriginal girl to live in his household, Marsden had made efforts to reach the Aboriginal people of the colony by bringing two young boys into his household. With the delay of the New Zealand mission Marsden proposed to the CMS that he retain at Parramatta the missionaries who were bound for New Zealand and put them to work in the "instruction of the natives of New Holland". This proposal was to "make some little establishment for the accommodation of our own natives, and those of the islands who may visit us". With these words Marsden expressed an interest in and a desire to reach the Aboriginal people with the gospel.

The problem was that when these efforts had failed to achieve their hoped for results Marsden was at a loss to know how to reach a people who, to his Western educated mind and cultural focus, demonstrated "no material wants". It was not that he had no interest in the Aboriginal people. It was more that when, blinkered by his Western cultural focus he was unable to make progress with them, he saw a more responsive people in the natives of New Zealand and directed his efforts there.

Marsden had a larger vision for the gospel when he saw missionary efforts taking place in strategic locations such as the African west coast and Malta. The response of the Aboriginal people in New South Wales to the limited efforts made by Marsden and others in bringing them the good news of salvation was small and disappointing. The greater potential from a people who Marsden felt would be more responsive, directed him to what he could see as a more strategic opportunity: to see the Māori first won for Christ. Strategically this could then open the way for the spread of the gospel among the less responsive Australian Aboriginal people.

## One great work of God

In speaking of the work of various missionary societies established in London, Marsden made the point that they were, "connected together as links in one grand chain, for the promotion of the gospel" (Sermon 34:8). This statement shows that in Marsden's thinking, strategically, in God's providence, these individual societies formed the one great work of God. There is not one mission to this people and another to that people. Each mission combines to form the one effort of promoting the gospel to the far flung ends of the earth. This "one grand chain" does not leave one people group behind but continues to link peoples throughout the world. Linking people of similar ethnic origins or of geographical proximity strategically opens the way for the gospel to spread back and forth across the globe.

Marsden believed the words of Jesus in the Great Commission gave "the missionaries of the gospel of peace a roving commission". He said that missionaries everywhere "have authority from the King of Kings to navigate all seas, to visit every island upon the bosom of the great deep, to traverse all continents" (Sermon 34:32). As a man who had been sent by the leading evangelicals of his day to take the "everlasting gospel" to the South Seas, Marsden took seriously his own place as a participant in this Commission.

Charles Grant of the East India Company, in a letter on 17 March 1791 to Charles Simeon, refers to Marsden as a "missionary". In his letter to Johnson, John Newton had implied as much when he encouraged Johnson to share the title, Apostle to the South Seas, with Marsden. Marsden saw himself not as a keeper of public morals in a prison colony but as a missionary taking the everlasting gospel to the people of the South Seas. To do this successfully, and in answer to his own prayer as he set out from his native shores in 1793, Marsden had to be a man of far reaching vision and strategic determination.

Colonial Secretary, J. T. Campbell, in his *Philo Free* letter, had not only accused Marsden of neglecting the Australian Aboriginals but had also declared motives of self-aggrandisement. The letter referred to Marsden as the "Christian Mahomet" averring that he was only looking for personal praise, honour, glory and profit in his efforts to take the gospel to the South Seas. On the contrary, Marsden was very clear about to whom the honour should go for the spread of the gospel around the world. By informing his congregation of the missionary work being done around the world by various Societies, Marsden was clear that this was God's work. The Societies and those who supported them were "secondary causes" in "what God is doing in the world" (Sermon 34:18). Likewise, when he wrote about successes of the missionary efforts in Tahiti, Marsden ascribed the triumph of this mission to the providence of God and expressed his views that those who spoke against the mission must now keep silent while the missionaries continue to do their work:

> Many, even sober-thinking men, for years viewed the Mission to the Islands with contempt; and considered it as the offspring of intemperate zeal. The mouths of gainsayers

must now be stopped, and infidels silenced. Nothing like this, as I have had occasion before to remark, has occurred since the days of the Apostles. We must look beyond all second causes, to the Great First Cause; and, while we do this, we must use such means as are within our reach, and follow closely the openings of Providence.[10]

## Criticisms of Wealth

Another criticism Marsden faced was that of Governor Brisbane who accused him of engaging in "trade cloaked under a surplice". Brisbane's belief was "that clergy, like government officials, should not indulge in private trade". Commissioner Bigge also criticised him for being "less sensible than he ought to have been to the impropriety of combining operations of a mercantile nature with those of his profession". If Marsden's sensibilities had been on what the perceptions of those who were keen to find fault with him might be, this criticism from Bigge might be just. However, such criticisms fail to understand Marsden's priorities and the place and importance of wealth juxtaposed to the importance of the gospel and his desire of using every means possible to create opportunity to spread the gospel.

Marsden's attitude to wealth can be seen in a small number of the sermons in the Moore College Collection. In Sermon 34:8, where he speaks of the works of the various missionary societies, he points out that the pious are giving their money to this work of spreading the gospel around the world.

---

10  Marsden in *Missionary Register* (1820), p.127.

the poor pious widow adds her mite and teaches her orphan school boy to spare his pocket money and to cast his weekly penny into the Lord's treasury. ... To the widows mite the rich and noble, the kings and queens of the earth give of their abundance

In 1814 Marsden had purchased the ship *Active* to aid the progress of the work of the Church Missionary Society in the South Seas. With this vessel he also engaged in trade with the Māori of New Zealand and other South Sea Islanders, giving rise to the criticism from Governor Brisbane and others that he was more interested in gaining wealth from his missionary enterprises than gaining the souls of men.

Marsden's intention in purchasing his own ship was to use it to enable a speedier means of bringing the gospel and civilisation to the Māori. It is unlikely that he seriously engaged in trade to expand his own wealth. In correspondence with the Church Missionary Society written on aboard the *Active* on his first journey to New Zealand, Marsden commended the welfare of his family to the Society should he not return, because, "much of my capital has been expended in the work". Not only had much of his capital been expended on this missionary cause but as Malcolm Falloon points out, "The reality was that the cost of buying and outfitting (let alone operating) the *Active* was more than Marsden could personally afford at the time".[11] Though he had become a wealthy man, his wealth was stretched to the limit. Nevertheless, Marsden used his wealth for the benefit of the missionary work which, in the event of an untimely death, would have left his family destitute

---

11  Falloon. '"Openings of Providence": The shaping of Marsden's missionary vision for New Zealand.' In *Launching Marsden's Mission*. p. 131.

without the intervention of the CMS for which he was undertaking this work.

Following the start of the New Zealand mission at Rangihoua Marsden recorded in his journal:

> as there was no timber at Rangheehoo fit for erecting the necessary buildings for the settlers, I determined to take the Active to the timber district … as this would save considerable expense and supply what was wanted at once.

With a view to saving both money and time, Marsden used his ship to establish this missionary presence in New Zealand.

## The Mission Delayed

The occasion of the mission to New Zealand was a significant one for the Māori chiefs and people who welcomed Marsden and his missionaries on one of the first European adventures into New Zealand waters since an attack on the company and destruction of the ship *Boyd* in December 1809.

On 10 March 1810 the *Sydney Gazette* reported that the *Boyd* had been "captured by the New Zealanders". The initial reports of the attack come from the Supercargo of the City of Edinburgh, Alexander Berry, who reported to Governor Macquarie that the *Boyd* had been taken in Whangaroa where on 31 December 1809 Berry had found the ship "burnt to the copper sheathing" and only four survivors: Mrs. Ann Morley, her infant daughter and another toddler, Elizabeth "Betsey" Broughton and a young cabin-boy, Thomas Davis. The rest of the crew had been killed and eaten. Such a shock was this attack to the Europeans that virtually all contact between the two peoples was suspended for five years.

On Christmas Day, 1814, five years after the attack on the *Boyd*, as Marsden and others rowed ashore at Rangihoua at the northern end of the Bay of Islands they were greeted by the Māori chiefs Korokoro, Ruatara and Hongi Hika dressed in British Regimentals provided to them by the Governor of New South Wales, Lachlan Macquarie. Their men were drawn up in regimental fashion under the British flag flying over New Zealand soil. This led Marsden to record in his journal that he considered this was "the signal for the dawn of civilization, liberty, and religion in that dark and benighted land" and then to express the hope that these British colours "would never be removed till the natives of that island enjoyed all the happiness of British subjects".

Behind this friendly, warm, welcoming scene lay years of hard work Marsden had put into establishing this mission to New Zealand. While official enquiries were progressing and apportioning blame after the *Boyd* incident which had so stalled meaningful contact between Westerner and Māori, Marsden was hard at work in the background, making his own enquiries and putting his own life at risk to bring reconciliation and peace between Māori tribes embroiled in the fallout of the incident.

Following Berry's report, official blame for the destruction of the *Boyd* and the murder of its crew had been laid at the feet of the Māori chief Te Pahi who was well known in Sydney, having been the first Māori chief to visit there. Between November 1805 and February 1806 Te Pahi had been the guest of Governor King and also an inquisitive attender at Marsden's church each Sunday. Yet as more evidence was gathered and a report from a Tahitian, who was considered to be impartial, was given, it became clear that Te Pahi had had nothing to do with the murders. He had arrived in Whangaroa the day after the initial attack and tried to rescue some of the crew who had climbed for safety into the rigging of the *Boyd*. As the Sydney Gazette reported in September 1810, "it appears that neither Tippahee [Te Pahi] nor his son Mytye [Matari] had any share in the barbarous acts committed by these sanguinary miscreants; but that the old chief had on the contrary endeavoured to preserve the lives of several of the crew". This report, however, came too late for Te Pahi. In retaliation for his alleged role in the *Boyd* incident, six whaling ships had sailed to Te Pahi's village in the Bay of Islands, some miles to the south of Whangaroa, and raided it. Te Pahi himself was wounded in this fight by bullets to the neck and chest and about sixty of his people killed. Marsden reports that Te Pahi received seven shots and died. A Māori woman who had given the whalers information about Te Pahi's whereabouts was taken to Port Jackson for her protection where she was interviewed by Marsden who then reported to the Church Missionary Society:

> I saw a New Zealand woman yesterday, who [arrived in the *Perseverance*] and she related the melancholy Story to me. The cause of this misfortune is not yet exactly known; as the natives had, at all times, previous to this Affair, been kind and attentive to our people. It is generally believed here that we were the first Aggressors. [...] I believe it will be found that we have treated the New Zealanders with the greatest injustice. It is much to be lamented that Englishmen should be such Savages as they often are, when amongst poor Heathen whom they imagine they have in their power.

Considering the varying accounts of why the *Boyd* had been attacked, Marsden came to the conclusion that it was because of the ill treatment given by ship's masters to the natives of the

South Seas. But things had gone into turmoil amongst the New Zealanders as well. With the death of Te Pahi at the hands of the Europeans for his alleged involvement, the people of the Bay of Islands declared war on the people of Whangaroa. Marsden recorded, "This most awful calamity extinguished at once all hopes of introducing the Gospel into that country". Not to be deterred from his goal however, Marsden set about to determine the truth and to bring reconciliation between all involved.

It was five years after the *Boyd* incident that Marsden finally arrived in New Zealand. He set about to bring peace between the warring tribes. In late December, 1814, landing at Whangaroa, the site of the destruction of the *Boyd* and her crew, Marsden spoke to the chiefs. He determined from them the facts surrounding, and the reasons for their attack on the *Boyd*. There was much discussion late into the night about the consequences of the attack, particularly how it had affected relationships amongst the New Zealanders themselves. With an assurance from the chiefs that they no longer wanted to fight and that they were ready to make peace Marsden recorded in his journal:

> When these ceremonies were over, I expressed my hope that they would have no more wars, but from that time would be reconciled to each other. Duaterra, Shunghie, and Koro Koro shook hands with the chiefs of Wangaroa, and saluted each other as a token of reconciliation by joining their noses together. I was much gratified to see these men at amity once more.

Marsden, Nicholas and Hongi from the Bay of Islands stayed on shore and slept on the beach among the people of Whangaroa. Marsden, with feelings he could not express, wondered at the "mysteries of Providence" as he lay down that night "surrounded by cannibals, who had massacred and devoured our countrymen". With such acts of trust, Marsden felt ready to bring his message of reconciliation between humankind and God just a few days later on Christmas Day in the Bay of Islands.

He based his sermon to the Māori people that day on Luke 2:10, "Behold, I bring you glad tidings of great joy". Sermon Two in the Moore College collection is on the same passage. In it Marsden says, "He [Jesus] came to bring about an immediate reconciliation between God and humans". No doubt, as he thought of these words in preparation for the mission to New Zealand and what he might say on Christmas Day 1814, Marsden had high hopes that the gospel message would bring about reconciliation between Westerner and Māori and between Māori and Māori.

## Ruatara

The mission to New Zealand would not have happened the way it did without Marsden's Māori friend. The young chief Ruatara had become an intimate friend of Marsden. He may have accompanied his uncle Te Pahi when he visited the colony of New South Wales in 1805 and made the acquaintance of Marsden. It may be that on this occasion Ruatara had been counted as one of Te Pahi's sons. The *Sydney Gazette* reported that Te Pahi arrived in Port Jackson with four sons and departed with five!

In 1814, in preparation for his mission to New Zealand, Marsden wrote to Ruatara whom he "had known nine years before", indicating that Ruatara may well have been in the company of his uncle in 1805. Certainly Ruatara arrived in Sydney on board the *Argo* on 20 September 1806 and departed on the *Albion* on 12 October of that year and it is likely that Marsden, having been impressed with the New Zealanders, met Ruatara on this occasion even if he had not been with his uncle a year earlier.

Marsden again encountered Ruatara on his return voyage from England in 1809 when the young man, in an appalling state of bodily infirmity, was nursed back to health by Marsden. Their friendship was cemented on this voyage. Marsden took the opportunity to learn the Māori language and, when the ship finally arrived in Port Jackson in February 1810, Ruatara spent the next nine months living as part of Marsden's household before leaving New South Wales on board the *Frederick* in November of that year.

The master of the *Frederick* was not a man of his word and despite sailing frustratingly close to Ruatara's home at the northern end of the Bay of Islands in the North Lands of New Zealand, so that his people were in sight, finally abandoned him and his fellow countrymen on Norfolk Island. With the providential arrival of the *Ann* at Norfolk, Ruatara was given passage back to Port Jackson and again came under the hospitality of Marsden and his family. Marsden records that Ruatara "had been about three years in my family" over this time before he was finally able to make passage back to New Zealand on board the *Ann* after her next return from England.

Being conscious of the importance of his proposed mission to New Zealand, Marsden sent his ship the *Active* to the Bay of Islands to bring Ruatara and the other chiefs to Sydney to accompany him on the voyage back to New Zealand. After some misgivings about the impact on his people of this missionary adventure to his native land, Ruatara was assured by Marsden that he would pull out of the mission if that is what the young chief wanted.

## Finally Underway

With Ruatara's mind at ease the *Active* left Port Jackson. The voyage proceeded and the ship arrived at Rangihoua, Ruatara's land in the north of the Bay of Islands, just before Christmas after Marsden's encounter with the people of Whangaroa noted above. In preparation for the Christmas Day service on Sunday, 25 December 1814, Ruatara spent most of the day enclosing about an acre of ground in which he built a pulpit and prayer desk. Marsden records in his journal that all this was at Ruatara's own initiative. Canoes were placed upside down as seats for the Europeans with the Māori men flanking them and the women and children and others encircling the whole. The service began with the singing of the "Old Hundred Psalm". Marsden then read the service with the Māori following the Europeans' lead and the direction of Korokoro. Marsden then preached on the text of Luke 2:10, "Behold I bring you glad tidings of great joy".

While most historians believe that what Marsden said was dutifully translated by Ruatara, there is a strong case to be made that Marsden spoke in the Māori language and Ruatara was prevailed upon to explain those parts of the Christian message his fellow countrymen did not understand.

Marsden had learnt the language from Ruatara on his return voyage to New South Wales from England in 1809 so that they conversed in the Māori language daily. Reading Marsden's account of his first voyage to New Zealand it is clear that in his first contact with the people of the North Cape, Marsden communicated with their chief in Māori. He relates the conversation and the pleasantries. Knowing that Marsden could speak the language, it is clear that he was speaking to this chief in the Māori language. His journal goes on:

I explained to the Chief the object of our Voyage, and enformed him that the *Active* would continue to visit them from time, to time, and Messrs Kendall, Hall and King would settle at the Bay of Islands for the general benefit of their Country. I also gave him a printed Copy of Governor McQuarries Instructions to Masters of Vessels relative to them; I explained their meaning which he comprehended and much approved of and directed him to shew these instructions to all the Captns of Vessels that touched their [sic] as they would be a protection to them.

It is clear from this account that Marsden was speaking to the chief in his own language. He explained Macquarie's Instructions to Masters of Vessels because the instructions were written in English. And so the chief was instructed by Marsden to show these instructions to any ship's master who might touch there.

It is most likely, with the language under his belt and a solemn sense of taking the gospel to the New Zealanders for the first time, Marsden would have attempted to communicate the Christian message on that Christmas Day in 1814 in the language of the local people. He reported in his 1809 journal, after he had learned the language from Ruatara, that he could make himself clearly understood in the Māori language. He wrote in his journal of Christmas 1814 that "The natives reported to Duaterra (Ruatara) that they could not understand what I meant". His use of the word "meant" rather than "said" is of significance in that, if he was speaking in the Māori language, he may have been speaking with an accent that made it difficult for the listeners to understand or he may have been speaking with awkward grammar or simply that he was communicating concepts so new to the hearers that they needed further explanation.

Furthermore, if Marsden had been preaching in English there would have been no need for "the natives to report to Ruatara that they did not understand". If Marsden had been preaching in a foreign language (English), their lack of understanding would have been expected and a report to their chief of their lack of understanding would be redundant.

John Nicholas, who accompanied Marsden on this voyage, kept a journal of events which he later published as *A Narrative of a voyage to New Zealand*. What he says in this narrative about Marsden's sermon is also instructive. Nicholas recorded on page 205 that Marsden spoke "through the medium of Duaterra" who "was ready enough to act as interpreter". This accords with Marsden's statement that the people did not understand his meaning. Nicholas wrote that Ruatara acted as an "interpreter" not a "translator", a distinction nuanced enough to possibly be of no significance, but interesting enough to lend weight to the theory that Ruatara did not act as a translator of Marsden's sermon, but interpreted the meaning when his people found Marsden's Māori words difficult to understand.

In fact Nicholas records that so interested in the message of "the only true God" were the New Zealanders that they had "several importunate questions ... regarding the minute particulars of the subject". This describes a situation where new and interesting things are being heard for the first time and those hearing are keen to understand. It hardly describes a situation of deception as expressed by the modern New Zealand scholar, Prof. James Belich.[12] Citing no evidence, Belich makes the assertion that

---

12 James Belich. *Making Peoples: A History of the New Zealanders from Polynesian Settlement to the End of the Nineteenth Century.* Auckland: Penguin, 1996.

Ruatara did not faithfully translate Marsden's sermon but simply encouraged his people to make like they were paying attention as Marsden spoke because they would profit greatly by association with Marsden and the British.

John King was also present on the beach in Rangihoua on Christmas Day 1814 when Marsden preached, and in a letter the following February to the Rev. Daniel Wilson said, "The first Sunday that Mr. Marsden preached on shore Duaterra (Ruatara) made him a pulpit. After the sermon Mr. Marsden asked him to explain it to the natives that were present". This accords with Marsden's account that the New Zealanders did not understand his meaning and that Ruatara was prevailed upon, not to act as translator, but to explain what Marsden meant.

One final account of Marsden's sermon will suffice to make the point. Mrs. E. M. Dunlop, writing for the Centenary of the event stated, "... prayers were said and lessons read, the service of the Church of England being followed and in a manner translated and explained with the assistance of Ruatara. Then Mr. Marsden gave out the text: 'Behold, I bring unto you glad tidings of great joy.' He told the story of the day, in all its grandeur and simplicity, and Ruatara made efforts to explain the subject of the sermon". This account, written one hundred years after the event and giving no references for its information, nevertheless makes a very clear statement that Ruatara translated and explained the service but simply explained the sermon. Clearly, the service of the Church of England would have been in English and in need of translation. The sermon, however, did not need translation, but it did need explanation. This account therefore also gives weight to the notion that Marsden preached in the Māori language but in such a way that his ideas needed further explanation.

We also know that Marsden, on a later occasion, taught the Māori some very sophisticated theological ideas in their own language. On Sunday 4 April 1830, he recorded that, "In the afternoon the natives met to be examined and catechized. I then spoke to them as well as I could in their own language". Where he wasn't sure of the correct word he referred to, "Mr King to explain the meaning". While this doesn't prove that he preached in Māori in 1814, it does show that Marsden had the ability to teach the Christian truths in Māori and that he used that ability when the occasion arose. We know that he learnt the language in 1809. It is reasonable to assume he used the language in his sermon in 1814 with the aid of Ruatara to explain his meaning as he did in his teaching in 1830 with the aid of Mr King to explain his meaning.

The three contemporary accounts of what happened as he preached on that Christmas Day in 1814, the account of Dunlop in celebration of the Centenary, and the fact that Marsden had a facility in the language make it most likely Marsden made some attempt at communicating his Christian message in the language of the New Zealanders.

What Marsden actually said on that Christmas Day is of great interest and a number of hopes have been expressed at various times that it might be possible to publish the sermon to mark various times of memorial or celebration. Among Marsden's many extant sermons, two are on the passage from which Marsden preached on Christmas Day 1814 – Luke 2:10. A third sermon begins on another passage but then turns to Luke 2:10. All of these sermons are in the Moore College collection.

It is known that Marsden also on occasion preached extempore. J. B. Marsden reports, "In his later years, when he was no longer able to read his sermons, he preached extempore". In some of his written sermons, which are in the main written out in full, there are notes to himself to "expand this" indicating that at this point in the sermon he would extemporise during the delivery. If Marsden wrote out the sermon he preached on that Christmas Day in the Bay of Islands it is probably lost to us. But it is most likely that this sermon was preached extempore. This is the expressed opinion of his granddaughter, Elizabeth Betts. Her mother, Martha, Marsden's youngest daughter, accompanied Marsden in his old age on his seventh and last voyage to New Zealand in 1837.

Some modern scholars believe that Marsden did not preach a sermon at all. They are emphatic that "in the Māori world of Rangihoua there was no sermon on 25 December 1814". Curiously, they believe, incorrectly, that because Marsden was speaking in English, and therefore the New Zealanders didn't understand his words, there was therefore no sermon. Their point is that Marsden spoke, the people didn't understand, therefore there was no sermon. Now if this is the sole criterion by which we determine what a sermon is, I beg to suggest that there are very few sermons ever preached at all! If a sermon is regarded as not preached because some in the congregation have not understood the preacher, then there have been very few sermons ever preached. On the contrary, Marsden did preach a sermon that morning, on the words from Luke 2:10, "Behold I bring you glad tidings of great joy". Whether or not the listeners, be they New Zealander, colonizer, or missionary, understood his meaning does not make it any less a sermon.

These scholars also follow the mistaken idea that Ruatara did not dutifully translate his friend's words on that occasion. It seems they do not know the fact that Marsden had learnt the language in 1809 and that he had Māori living with him at Parramatta from the beginning of 1810 until he first travelled to New Zealand in

1814. They say, "Marsden could understand neither the people's questions nor Ruatara's words".[13]

This speculation that Ruatara did not faithfully translate Marsden's words is just as curious as the belief that Marsden did not preach a sermon. We know that Marsden learnt the language from Ruatara so that they could carry on daily conversations and Marsden could make himself understood. If Marsden preached in English, the fact of his facility in the Māori language remains. He would have understood any translation Ruatara would have given. If Ruatara was translating from English to Māori Marsden would have understood what he was saying and, if he had not been making some attempt to explain what Marsden was saying, but rather was simply telling his people to pay attention because with him great prosperity would come through trade, Marsden would have been aware that his friend was not faithfully translating his message.

In the end we must reject the notion that Ruatara was deceptive on that occasion as he aided Marsden in the proclamation of the Christian gospel. It is quite unlikely that Ruatara would have tried to deceive his long-time friend in this way.

The idea that Ruatara, who had spent about three years living with Marsden in Parramatta, was only interested in material benefits ignores Ruatara's meticulous preparations for this Christmas Day gathering. It implies that the Christian influence on Ruatara over his nine years of friendship with Marsden had had no effect. It further implies that the preparations Ruatara made by enclosing about an acre of ground and building a pulpit for Marsden to preach from were an elaborate deception. More than

---

13   Alison Jones and Kuni Jenkins. *Words between Us – He Korero First Maori – Pakeha Conversations on Paper*. Wellington. Huia Publishers. 2011. p. 83.

this, the implication that Ruatara had no interest in the Christian gospel, but was only interested in gaining wealth through trade, flies in the face of Māori oral tradition.

The Rt. Rev. Te Kitohi Pikaahu, Anglican Bishop of the Northlands, New Zealand says that oral tradition has it that Ruatara prepared his people to receive the message Marsden was to bring. They were not expecting him to talk about trade and material benefits, but responded with song and dance to Marsden's sermon as the harbinger of a new season of the gospel being planted amongst them. Bishop Kitohi says that following Marsden's sermon the Māori present responded immediately in song and dance with these words:

> It is moving; it is shifting
> It is moving; it is shifting
> Look to the open sea of Waitangi
> Spread before us
> like the shinning cuckoo
> It is good, all is well
> Change is coming soon,
> is on the horizon
> It is good, all is well,
> let peace be established

In explanation, Bishop Kitohi says that the "shinning cuckoo" "is the gospel messenger that points to something that is coming … And what is coming? The power of the gospel is coming to establish the Kingdom of God". In response to Marsden's sermon, "there was a new creation, there was a new people established, and why Ngāpuhi (the people of the Northland) had the dance of joy on receiving the gospel, following the sermon". Bishop Kitohi's understanding of the occasion, derived from Māori oral tradition, is that the local Māori in 1814 were well prepared to hear the Christian gospel, understood the message that was proclaimed by Marsden, and responded to this message with expressions of hope that peace and the Kingdom of God was now established among them.[14]

## The Sermon

It is interesting to speculate what Marsden might have said on that occasion of the first New Zealand sermon on Christmas Day 1814 as he preached from Luke 2:10 in the Māori language with the assistance of his friend Ruatara. It is possible, with the three sermons we have on the passage, to work out what Marsden might have said on that occasion by examining what we know he did say on these three other occasions when he preached on that passage.

In Marsden's three sermons on Luke 2:10 there are eight themes or threads of thought common to each of them. We may assume Marsden used these common thoughts each time he preached on this passage and so be able to reconstruct what he might have said on Christmas Day 1814. Putting these eight themes together we can safely say that on Christmas Day 1814, on the beach at Rangihoua at the northern end of the Bay of Islands, New Zealand, when he preached the first Christian sermon, in the Māori language, Marsden made the following points:

---

14 See Bishop Kitohi's chapter in: Allan Davidson, Stuart Lange, Peter Lineham, Adrienne Puckey (Eds) *Te Rongopai 1814 'Takoto te pai!' Bicentenary reflections on Christian beginnings and developments in Aotearoa New Zealand*. General Synod Office. Auckland. 2014.

1. The birth of Christ is the most important event the world has ever seen.
2. It is good tidings of great joy for all people.
3. This event has been long and anxiously expected by the faithful.
4. Those who are awaiting a temporal messiah will be disappointed because this Messiah brings spiritual blessings.
5. This event has been announced with great rejoicing by the angels of heaven who have declared a Saviour for mankind.
6. This Messiah was not born in a palace, but a stable, making him accessible to all people.
7. This is the superior Saviour because he defeats the Evil One and saves from Hell.
8. Now is the time to follow this Saviour because you may not be alive next Christmas season.[15]

On this occasion Marsden called on his congregation – missionary, settler, and Māori alike – to understand that the message of this day was the greatest message for all humankind. The announcement of a saviour brought great rejoicing in heaven and on earth and called upon all people to respond. Thus began the Christianising of New Zealand.

---

15   For a full reconstruction of what Marsden might have said in his sermon using these eight points see http://alltogether.co.nz/wp-content/uploads/2013/07/Christmas-Day-1814.pdf This reconstruction uses Marsden's own words from these three sermons with very little editing.

CHAPTER FOUR

# MARSDEN AND MACQUARIE

THE RELATIONSHIP BETWEEN Marsden and Governor Lachlan Macquarie provides a special focus in understanding Marsden. The relationship between the parson and the Governor did not get off to a good start despite the high expectations of like-mindedness and it continued to deteriorate until it was entirely severed by Macquarie in 1818.[16]

It is to be regretted that two men of extraordinary ability, energy and conviction, having generous hopes of working for the same cause of establishing a moral and prosperous society, could so antagonise each other that their relationship finally broke down completely.

---

16  On 8 January 1818 Macquarie summonsed Marsden to a meeting at which the Rev. William Cowper, the Colonial Secretary J. T. Campbell and Lieutenant John Watts were present. Macquarie informed Marsden that he now viewed him, 'as the head of a seditious low cabal and consequently unworthy of mixing in private society or intercourse with me, I beg to inform you, that I never wish to see you except on public duty.' See Macquarie's *Journal*. 1816–1818, ML. A773. Commissioner Bigge in his report on the state of the colony said of this dismissal, "The ... points in which the magisterial office has suffered in New South Wales, are the loss of the services of the Rev. Mr. Marsden, and the circumstances that attended his dismissal".

In his preaching Marsden's major focus was not on creating a moral society but an eschatological one, a people who might bring social renewal by their own personal renewal in Christ, but still a people whose final hope was in heaven. His relationship with Macquarie highlights how Marsden was not successful in communicating this focus. As the "blinkered visionary" he had high hopes that his evangelical message would bring about an improvement of morals in a people who looked to heaven, but he could not see how best to communicate this message with the result that he left some confusion as to the thrust of what his message was.

In one sense it was inevitable that two such men should clash, but neither man was more at fault than the other in their tensions. Both had inconsistencies. Both made mistakes, misunderstanding each other's intentions. As strong minded men, faults lay on both sides. Macquarie never understood Marsden and took hasty actions based on inadequate information. At the same time Marsden, with exclusivist views and an inability to fully communicate his evangelical Christianity to a secular society, is not without blame for the breakdown in relationships with the Governor.

Marsden's very difficult relationship with Macquarie highlights the difficulties Marsden faced over a significant period with regard to his reputation in New South Wales. The controversies that arose for Marsden during Macquarie's time set the agenda for many of his opponents so that to a very real extent those controversies follow him to this day and are accepted without further analysis by many modern writers. The beginnings of Marsden's reputation as a harsh magistrate, however, were prior to Macquarie's time in the colony, despite Marsden's own statement that the charge of being a harsh magistrate was first made in 1817.[17]

Marsden and his fellow magistrate Atkins received censure for a notorious incident involving the punishment of an Irish convict, Paddy Galvin, in September 1800. It was suspected that the Irish convicts were planning an insurrection and had stolen and hidden some pikes which were to be later used as weapons. It was believed that Galvin had knowledge of the hiding place of these pikes, but he refused to divulge the information. Marsden and Atkins therefore sentenced the poor wretch to a flogging of 300 lashes each day until he gave up the information.

Such torture was seen to be harsh and illegal even by the standards of those days and greatly undermined Marsden's reputation. While Marsden and Atkins can be criticised for their sentencing of Galvin their appointment as magistrates highlights an issue that is rarely discussed by historians. These men were not qualified in law and yet they were expected to administer law and punishment in a penal colony.

## A difficult relationship – the Beginnings

From the beginning of his ministry in New South Wales Marsden's constant refrain in his sermons was against the immorality of the colonists. His first sermon in the colony was about Sabbath breaking.[18] His sermons have many denunciations against drunkenness and immorality. In Sermon 4:3 in the Moore College Collection

---

17  See, Samuel Marsden. *Answer to Certain Calumnies* p. 34. Marsden declares that the charge of severity as a magistrate was first made against him by Macquarie in a dispatch to Bathurst dated 4 December, 1817.

18  John Buxton Marsden and James Drummond. *Life and Work of Samuel Marsden*. London: Whitcombe and Tombs Limited, 1913. p.10.

Marsden states, "many of us have lived in the open and avowed violation of his laws. In Sabbath breaking, in profanation of God's name, in theft, in adultery, in drunkenness and every vice".

And yet, as much as he inveighed against immorality, Marsden had very little success in persuading the colonists to turn from their wickedness and live the Christian life. Some believe that Marsden's acceptance of a magistrate's position was an attempt to have a more direct influence over the people. Yet, while he certainly desired to raise the standard of moral behaviour in the colony, Marsden has said that his roles as preacher on the one hand and magistrate on the other had two distinct purposes.

As a preacher he desired to see people fit for heaven and evidence of this would be seen in a moral life here on earth. He believed the use of corporal punishment to persuade people of the truth of the gospel was abhorrent. In Sermon 45:7 Marsden says, "It is the force of persuasion we are to use [for the conversion of souls], not the force of penal statutes. Such compulsion as that is as abhorrent from reason as it is from religion".

The role of the magistrate was to see good order and government established in the colony. In the Moore College Collection in Sermon 23 Marsden compares the offices of preacher and magistrate. On page 1 he says, "The office of ministers is to preach the gospel of Christ". And on page 4, "The office of magistrates is to do all in their power for the suppression of iniquity". And yet while these are two distinct offices, it is also the role of the preacher, in proclaiming the duties of gospel obedience, not to pass by the duties, "which pertain to us as members of civil communion". (23:3)

In 1807 Marsden went to England to recruit more teachers and clergy for the colony and missionaries for his planned mission to New Zealand. On his return to the colony on 27 February 1810, and having had small success in his recruitment drive in England, Marsden found that the newly appointed Governor, Lachlan Macquarie, was already at work addressing the immorality Marsden had preached so vehemently against.

As it turned out, Macquarie was equally horrified at the immorality in the colony and just under a month after his swearing in as Governor, Macquarie decreed, on 27 January 1810, that anyone breaking the laws on Sabbath keeping would be arrested. A further month on, on 24 February, and just three days before Marsden landed back in Port Jackson, Macquarie expressed his displeasure at "the scandalous and pernicious custom" of those "living together unsanctioned by the legal ties of matrimony". It is no surprise, therefore, that in June 1813 Marsden's oldest daughter Ann described Macquarie as "a great friend of the gospel" and praised his "great improvements in the Colony".[19] These decrees, however, did not give Macquarie any greater success in improving the moral behaviour of the colonists than Marsden had. Neglect of the Sabbath was still rife. Simeon Lord, an emancipist and well regarded by Macquarie, did not regularise his living arrangements until 1814.

Despite these agreements on the nature of moral behaviour in the colony, Marsden and Macquarie found themselves in conflict on a number of issues, not least of which was the role of emancipists in the colony.[20] Marsden was not alone in opposing Macquarie on

---

19 Ann Marsden to Mrs. Stokes, 18 June 1813. Mackaness. *Some Private Correspondence*. pp. 48-49.
20 A. T. Yarwood. 'Marsden, Samuel (1765–1838)', *Australian Dictionary of Biography*. Volume 2. Melbourne University Press. 1967. pp 207-212. Note also the introduction to *Certain Calumnies* where Marsden focused his attention on the Governor's 'new theoretical system of policy' where, had he 'duly weighed this subject' (p.4), would have understood that a system to 'unite the free and the convict population in one body' (p. 2) would never succeed because it was against 'the inherent principles of mankind' (p.4).

the issue of what responsibilities should be given to emancipists but, surprisingly, Marsden's mentor, William Wilberforce held an opposite view and attempted mediation between Marsden and Macquarie.

In March 1814 Wilberforce wrote to Macquarie saying, "I am sorry Mr. Marsden differs from us on this subject. He is a very worthy man ... (but) he is liable to error ... I think his opinions erroneous in this instance".[21] And to Marsden a week later Wilberforce wrote that he had discussed the matter with several friends "and the result is that we all, without a single exception are of the opinion that persons who came out as convicts, should *after giving sufficient proofs of their having amended their ways,* be admissible to office".[22]

Even so, Ellis, Macquarie's biographer, informs us that Wilberforce, in writing to Macquarie, could not doubt "that attention to the religious and moral state of the colony would in a few years produce improvement which men would scarcely anticipate", and that the Governor's encouragement of marriage and of domestic virtues would be of "unspeakable benefit to everyone in the rising settlements".[23]

Marsden identified the difficulties between himself and Macquarie as beginning very early in their relationship, in 1810, with his request to the Governor to be excused from serving as a commissioner of the turnpike road that Macquarie intended to build from Sydney

---

21 Yarwood. *A.D.B.*
22 M. H. Ellis. *Lachlan Macquarie.* Sydney: Angus & Robertson. 1952. p. 330. The problem with Lord was that he had not 'amended his ways' morally in that he was still living in a *de facto* relationship until 1814, some four years after Macquarie had appointed him, alongside Marsden and another emancipist, Andrew Thompson, as a Commissioner to a proposed toll road from Sydney to the Hawkesbury.
23 Ellis. *Macquarie.* p. 203.

to the Hawkesbury. Marsden only discovered through the *Sydney Gazette* that he, along with two emancipists, Andrew Thompson and Simeon Lord, had been appointed. Marsden expressed his concern to Macquarie, pointing out to the Governor that while on the one hand he made public proclamations to encourage moral behaviour in the colony, he had now appointed two men who were living in open relationship with women to whom they were not married. In a letter of 2 April Marsden denied there was any personal animosity towards the Governor, but that he could not sit with two men of such immoral character in an official capacity.[24]

This letter indicates that Marsden's objections were not of an exclusivist nature but of a moral one. He did not state that he refused to sit as a Commissioner with these men because they had been convicts. His objection to their appointment was because they were living with women to whom they were not married. In his *Answer to Certain Calumnies* however, Marsden focuses solely on the issue of Lord and Thompson having been former convicts as the reason for his refusal to sit with them as a Commissioner.[25] In consideration of his objections to sitting with Lord and Thompson, Macquarie told Marsden that he found his objection to be gross insubordination, informing the chaplain that if he had not had his commission changed from a military to a civil appointment on his recent trip back to England, he would be now facing a court martial.[26]

Both Thompson and Lord were later appointed magistrates to

---

24 The letter of 2 April 1810 can be found in the appendix to the *Bigge report*, ML. Box 12. p. 347. This explanation highlights the misunderstandings and lack of communication between Marsden and Macquarie. Marsden's evidence: ML. Box 8. pp. 3373-3386.
25 *Certain Calumnies*. pp. 4-6.
26 *Certain Calumnies*. pp. 5-6

the bench in Sydney. In letters to the Archbishop of Canterbury on 2 May 1810 and to Wilberforce on 27 July 1810 Marsden wrote, "It is not consistent with morality, religion, or sound policy, to nominate men magistrates, who have been convicts and who are still living openly in profligacy".[27] In this correspondence, written shortly after his first altercation with Macquarie, Marsden states clearly that his objections were twofold, namely Thompson and Lord were emancipists and that they were living with women to whom they were not married. In his letters to Macquarie and to Marsden, Wilberforce seems to have ignored Marsden's second objection.

Despite the infamous incident involving Paddy Galvin, noted above, Marsden believed that his reputation as a severe magistrate arose, unjustly, from Macquarie.[28] It is surprising, as Marsden points out in his letter to Wilberforce, that Macquarie who had made such clear statements against men and women living together without the sanction of marriage, should then appoint such men to public office.

As Macquarie stood on his authority and demanded unquestioning obedience, there was never an explanation for his inconsistency in making a decree that men in official positions should not live in *de facto* relationships and yet appointing two such men to be commissioners of a major infrastructure project. Likewise, there is no explanation for inconsistency in Marsden that while giving no inch in his obstinate stand on principle and opposing the Governor nevertheless preached that God enjoins upon his people "a peaceable and quiet subjection to earthly governors as God's ministers". (Sermon 27:1)

---

27 Marsden to Wilberforce, 27 July 1810. *Bonwick Transcripts* (Missionary) Box 49, p. 85. Cited by Yarwood in *Great Survivor*. p. 130.
28 *Certain Calumnies*. pp. 4,6,37.

## Death of Ellis Bent

There were more incidents, beside those already noted, that led to tension between Marsden and Macquarie. Marsden's refusal to read public proclamations from the pulpit and his use of the Goode Psalms[29] in public worship were cause for not inconsiderable tension. Macquarie's mistaken belief that Marsden was responsible for complaints made to the Home Office about his administration led to their final falling out on 8 January 1818. However, the sermon Marsden preached following the death of the Judge Advocate, Mr Ellis Bent, provided opportunity for Macquarie to give Marsden a public dressing down. Bent died on 10 November, 1815. Macquarie took the sermon as a personal insult, believing Marsden had used the opportunity to inveigh against him publicly.[30]

At the outset it must be stated that in all of the sermons in various collections there is not one where Marsden directly addresses any of the controversial issues he faced. There are certainly allusions and a critical eye may read more into Marsden's words than he intended, but Marsden never used the pulpit to justify himself directly against any particular criticism. When preaching on the role of magistrates, for example, which he did in Sermons 23 and 56, Marsden does not seek to defend himself from accusations of harshness as a magistrate nor to attack his accusers. He confines his comments to the biblical text and its application. Likewise in

---

29  In 1811 The Rev William Goode published his first edition of "An Entire New Version of the Book of Psalms". Goode was a founding member of the CMS and, according to Yarwood, it was in the study of his Rectory at Blackfriars that the proposal by Marsden of the establishment of a mission to New Zealand was first agreed to by the CMS committee. See *Great Survivor* p. 115.

30  The sermon is held by the Mitchell Library, Sydney. *Marsden Papers*. Mitchell Library C244, pp. 17-40.

Sermon 76, in speaking on a Christian's proper use of wealth, and encouraging his congregation to give generously to the relief of the survivors of Sydney's first major shipping disaster in the wreck of the barque *Edward Lombe* on Middle Head on 25 August, 1834, Marsden does not defend or excuse himself for the wealth he had amassed. Neither does he use the opportunity to attack those who had declared his mercantile and farming interests to be in conflict with his calling as a minister of the gospel.

It is therefore difficult to surmise that in his sermon following the death of the Judge Advocate in 1815, Marsden set out to attack Macquarie and his administration. If he had done so it would have been contrary to the nature of all his preaching over a period of some twenty years or more. Macquarie did, however, take great exception to what Marsden said in this sermon about Bent.

The sermon Marsden preached following the death of the Judge Advocate, Ellis Bent, like many of his sermons, followed the outline of the Rev Charles Simeon of Cambridge. It is also clear that he has followed the intent of the outline faithfully. These facts make it difficult to believe that the main thrust of this sermon was even a veiled attack upon the Governor.

For this sermon Marsden has followed Simeon's outline number 421 with a title of "The use of covenanting with God"[31] which is based on the text of 2 Chronicles 29:10-11. A note in the text of Simeon's outline indicates it was written in response to a Royal Decree calling for a Fast Day in March 1798.

---

31  Simeon. *Horae Homileticae*. Vol. 4. pp. 181-185.

## A Public Dressing Down

Much has been made of Macquarie's public dressing down of Marsden following this sermon. Some think Marsden used the opportunity to speak against Macquarie's administration but others think he was reprimanded by Macquarie for having spoken with too high a regard for Bent and thereby was blaspheming.

However, in its major thrust, following Simeon's outline, the sermon was not about Bent. It appears to be a sermon preached in the ordinary round of Sunday sermons by Marsden, and his reference to Bent is only one illustration of several calamities Marsden named that he saw as indicative of God's anger against the colony for the people's neglect of Him and his standards.

Macquarie's biographer, M. H. Ellis, has Marsden "thundering" from the pulpit that "God had taken from the Israelites an upright judge".[32] How Ellis can hear down over a century of time a "thundering" voice has more to do with his own imaginings and clear prejudice against Marsden than any reality. It can equally be imagined that the words were delivered in a soft, even melancholy voice as Marsden was speaking about his friend who had died. Marsden's actual words were, "God in his anger often removed from the Israelites an upright Judge or King".[33]

In the context of the sermon as a whole, Marsden was calling upon his congregation to consider a number of current events he declared were indicative of God's anger against the sinfulness of the people of the colony. These events included a drought, crops failing and cattle dying in the fields. Marsden added to these events the recent, untimely death of the young Judge Advocate. He called

---

32  Ellis. *Lachlan Macquarie*. p.384.
33  Bent Sermon p. 10.

upon the congregation to repent of any sins that may have been causing the anger of God to "wax hot" against them.

It is well known that by the time of Bent's death in late 1815 Macquarie did not get along with either Marsden or Bent.[34] One report of Macquarie's complaint is that he sought to defend God rather than himself. The report states that Macquarie accused Marsden of speaking too highly of Bent and was therefore blaspheming. But if Macquarie thought that speaking too highly of the deceased Judge Advocate was a criticism of himself or his administration it is reasonable to expect that he would have said something like, "by speaking too highly of the Judge Advocate, who was an opponent of mine, you have attacked me and my administration", yet says nothing of the sort. Moreover, if the Governor saw it as his position to defend God, then it is the Governor who was seeking to attack the chaplain and his ministry by entering into an area of Marsden's expertise and openly criticising his preaching.

## The Sins of the People

Another comment about Macquarie's rebuke comes from Commissioner Bigge's report based on what Macquarie said to him about the incident and shows that blasphemy was not the Governor's concern. In a letter to Marsden Bigge reported:

> The Governor reproached Mr Marsden [not][35] for eulogising the Character of Mr Ellis Bent but for having declared in his

---

34 On Bent's relationship with Macquarie see, N. D. McLachlan, 'Macquarie, Lachlan (1762 – 1824)', *Australian Dictionary of Biography*. Volume 2. Melbourne University Press. 1967. pp 187-195 and C. H. Currey. 'Bent, Ellis (1783 – 1815)'. *Australian Dictionary of Biography*. Volume 1. Melbourne University Press. 1966. pp 87-92.
35 'not' is missing in this reference but the context demands it.

Sermon preached at Parramatta "that no greater calamity could befall a Country than the loss of an Upright Judge, and that no doubt the Sins of this Colony had been the cause of Mr Bent's death as a Chastisement from the Almighty for the Sins of the People."[36]

This account clearly states that Macquarie's complaint was not that Marsden had eulogized Bent too highly, but that Marsden had attributed the judge's death to a "Chastisement from the Almighty for the Sins of the People". Even though Bigge criticised Macquarie in his report, by quoting Macquarie's own words, Commissioner Bigge gives a more reliable account of Macquarie's complaint. In this scenario Macquarie was defending the people rather than either himself or God, but in making this criticism Macquarie has shown that he had misunderstood the thrust and intent of the sermon.

It is clear from the sermon context that Marsden did not have the Governor specifically in view in speaking about the death of the Judge Advocate. Rather, he was calling upon all the people of the colony to consider certain calamities that had recently befallen them and to examine their lives to see how they might repent of sinful behaviour. In doing this Marsden was faithfully following the intent of the Simeon outline he was reliant upon and was consistent with a genre of "Fast Days Sermons" where the Sovereign or Chief Minister called on the people to observe a Fast Day to call upon God that he might forgive the people of any sin and give them relief from their current suffering.

While there is no record of Macquarie having called a Fast Day at this time, and there is therefore no decree acting as a catalyst

---

36  J.T. Bigge to S. Marsden, 20 Jan 1821. Marsden Papers. p.50 at ML: C244.

for this sermon, the fact of the drought of late 1815 causing crop failure and the death of cattle was sufficient cause for Marsden to call on his congregation to examine themselves and to call upon God for mercy.[37]

## The real thrust

Simeon's outline, which Marsden used for the basis of his sermon following Bent's death, shows that the inspiration for writing the outline was a royal proclamation for the observance of a Fast-day in March 1798.[38] In the outline it is stated that the King had called the Fast Day in "consideration of the just and necessary war in which we are engaged … putting our trust in Almighty God that He will graciously bless our arms". Simeon then states, "surely the displeasure of God can scarcely ever be more strongly displayed, than it is in the calamities under which we now groan".[39] Marsden called on his congregation to be conscious of a number of calamities that had come upon them recently. Following Simeon's outline, Marsden said that such things were the means by which God often alerted His people to their sin. The proper response was to ponder these warnings and to examine one's own conscience to see if there were any sins of which they should repent.

Simeon's outline calls upon the people to repent and make a covenant with God because the calamities that have come upon them are indicative of God's wrath against them. Without

---

37 Fast Days were not unknown in the colony. Governor Gipps called a Fast Day for Friday 2 November, 1838 to which several preachers responded.
38 See King's Proclamation for a General Fast dated 24 January, 1798. The day set aside for the Fast was Wednesday, 7 March, 1798.
39 Simeon. *Horae Homileticae*. Vol. 4. p.183.

repentance they cannot hope to escape. With repentance there is nothing to fear. In following Simeon's outline Marsden has listed events he believed were signs of God's anger "waxed hot against" the people of the colony. In his sermon Marsden says on page 14:

> we have reason to apprehend that God is angry with us for our sins, from the rains being withheld, the earth not bringing forth its increase, our cattle dying with famine, and ourselves threatened with the same calamity which is God's usual method of punishing nations for their iniquities (and from God taking from us a just and upright judge.)[40]

He had earlier stated on page nine that these calamities were the evidence of God's anger against them:

These things are certain tokens that God's anger is waxed hot against us for our sins and none of us can tell what the end will be. We can expect no favour if we continue still to do wickedly. Marsden lamented the depravity that pervaded the colony and on page three listed the sins and wickedness so prevalent:

> There is no sin however serious which is not practised without remorse amongst us. Lying & perjury & theft, and whoredom, and blasphemy, and drunkenness, are daily committed amongst us.

He has left no-one out of his chastisement for ingratitude towards God and for obvious sin and reiterates that God has shown his

---

40 The words in parentheses are added above the line. This may indicate that Marsden had written this sermon in preparation for Sunday before Bent had died. He has then considered Bent's death as yet another calamity and so has added it as a further illustration.

displeasure with the behaviour of the people of the Colony by visiting upon them certain calamities. On page three Marsden says, "What ingratitude have we all shewn for mercies received". And on page nine:

> our sins are so public and so great. We declare our sins as Sodom. We hide them not. Surely the displeasure of God can scarcely ever be more ~~displade~~[41] strongly displayed than it is under the public calamities under which we now groan.

Marsden, following Simeon's outline, called upon the people of the colony to turn from their sin and rededicate themselves to God, being assured of eternal bliss if they so turn. "What should not we affect if we were all to turn unto God with sincerity? God would soon relieve our wants" (Page 15). He then invited his congregation directly to repent, "we now invite you to turn unto the Lord your God with weeping and with mourning" (Page 18) and on page twenty warns them of the consequences of not repenting with an assurance on page twenty-two that with true repentance God will give relief:

> With respect to us as a body of people, who can tell how soon the cloud that now hangs over us may burst. We have had loud warnings to repent, and of long continuance, and we may expect that God will increase our public calamities if we continue to increase our iniquities, and in the end cause us to feel all the evils of famine and general distress.
>
> Let us make a covenant with the Lord God of Israel. If we heartily engage in this duty we have nothing to fear. Were

---

41  Crossed out words in transcripts of Marsden's sermons are in the original.

such a covenant general amongst us God would soon remove his judgement. He would give us the early and the latter rain in their season.

Of those who turn to seek God, Marsden promised on page twenty three that they will know God as their refuge even if the calamities continue:

> Tho they may be involved in the general calamity they shall be comforted with the divine presence. Many are the afflictions of the righteous that the Lord delivereth them out of them all. They will always find him a present help in time of need. They need not then be agitated with fear on their own account with God's displeasure with the world, for tho the earth should be removed our God would still be their refuge, a very present help in time of need.

The thrust of this sermon shows that Marsden has been faithful to the intent of Simeon's outline and that he has addressed some very pressing issues within the colony, encouraging his congregation to think seriously about the spiritual implications involved for them of the current drought and its attendant calamities. His phrasing throughout has been inclusive, giving evidence of his pastoral concern for his people.

## The Significance of the Death of Ellis Bent

The mention of the death of the Judge Advocate in this sermon is understandable, particularly as it was more than likely Marsden's first address to his congregation after the funeral of Mr Bent. What would not be understandable would have been a total neglect of any mention of Bent and his recent passing. Moreover, Marsden was impressed with Bent's Christian commitment and understanding and held these out to his congregation as an example of godly living:

> With respect to the doctrines of the Christian religion I had many conversations with him, both before and during his last sickness (upon him). He searched the scriptures daily like the Bereans, to see whether these things were so. He was very anxious to know the way to glory. The Psalms of David afforded him much consolation, and also the Esiples *(sic)* of St. Paul. We had much conversation on these doctrines contained in these epistles a few days before his death. The word of God appeared to be very precious to him. (Pages 12-13)

The death of a man of Christian commitment and of high ranking in the colony at an early age[42] would have been the subject of some talk and maybe speculation about God's action. In the context of this sermon, therefore, it is understandable that Marsden had included Bent's recent death as another calamity that had befallen the people of the colony. Marsden's words were:

> I beg also to mention another (recent event) circumstance which I consider as a most serious calamity to the inhabitants of this Colony, and an awful token of the divine displeasure, viz. the death of our Judge Advocate. (Page 10)

Failing to understand the sermon, Macquarie has turned Marsden's words from, "a most serious calamity to the inhabitants of this

---

42  Bent was only 32 when he died.

Colony" to, "no doubt the Sins of this Colony had been the cause of Mr Bent's death".[43] In his pastoral care for the people Marsden was, however, careful in his choice of words. He did not say the sins of the colony had caused Bent's death. He said that Bent's death was a "most serious calamity to the inhabitants of this Colony" (Page 10).

Macquarie's complaint was simply that he thought Marsden had said that the death of Ellis Bent was caused by the sins of the people of the colony. In his own mind, and in those of his biographers and other historians, Macquarie may well have seen this as a criticism of himself, but to be consistent he should have also mentioned that he thought Marsden was saying that the sins of drunkenness, whoring and Sabbath breaking (sins which are a refrain in Marsden's sermons) were the cause of the calamities of drought, famine and crop failure, which Marsden had listed alongside the calamity of the death of an upright judge. As he did not do this the inevitable conclusion is that the Governor has allowed his ill feelings towards both Marsden and Bent to cloud his understanding and judgement and he has therefore made a wrongful accusation against the chaplain.

It is to be regretted that Macquarie's relationship with both Bent and Marsden had deteriorated to the extent that the Governor focussed on one point of the sermon, transgressed into the realm of the expertise of the preacher and missed the whole thrust of the sermon. Macquarie's complaint was that Marsden attributed Bent's death to the sins of the colony, an assertion that has missed the point of the sermon. That Macquarie has missed the point must lead us to also reject any assertion that Marsden inveighed "in scarcely veiled terms against Macquarie and his administration". As

---

43 *Marsden Papers*. ML. C 244. p. 50

the thrust of Marsden's sermon was the same as Simeon's outline, namely that God had visited certain calamities upon the people because of their sin, those who see a veiled attack on Macquarie in Marsden's sermon must also see a veiled attack on the King in Simeon's outline. As there is clearly no such treasonable intent in Simeon's outline it must lead us to the conclusion that those who attribute mal-intent to Marsden's words have, like the Governor, missed the thrust of the sermon and the careful wording Marsden has used.

## Marsden and Authority

Marsden understood that ministers had their responsibilities and governors and magistrates had their different responsibilities. These responsibilities might sometimes overlap and seem to be trying to achieve the same ends such as the reduction of immoral behaviour. Yet, as Marsden saw it, the minister's ultimate goal was to prepare people for heaven. The magistrate's or the governor's role was to maintain order in this world. There is, however, another level and responsibility unique to the minister as Marsden saw it. In Sermon 91:17 he has said:

> This subject speaks also powerfully to those who are messengers of God to a guilty world. It is at the peril of a minister's own soul if throw *(sic)* cowardice or sloth he neglect to warn men of their danger. They must like Elijah put themselves in the way of sinners and bear testimony for God against them. There is a duty laid upon them that is not imposed upon any other men in the world

Marsden believed that he had a unique authority from God. It is a duty "laid upon" ministers by God. They must stand in front of sinners and declare God's testimony against their sin. Marsden would have believed this authority to be greater authority than that of the Governor because it was from God and it had eternal consequences. He has stated that the minister will shrink from this responsibility at the peril of his own soul. Such belief, both in the authority he had from God and the danger to his own eternal salvation, would have given Marsden an unwavering determination that when he spoke about the things of God even the Governor was subject to his authority. Even if he had been personally upset by Macquarie's public dressing down he would not have doubted for one moment that what he had said in his sermon after Ellis Bent's death was anything but the truth, a truth that even Macquarie must submit to.

The *Sydney Gazette* reported in the month following Marsden's delivery of this sermon that the drought, which he had declared to be one indication of God's wrath against the people, had broken. It may well be that some folk had understood the intent of the sermon and repented of their sins and God had therefore relaxed his anger. This is speculation, but it is the outcome Marsden was seeking in preaching this sermon and would indicate that the sermon had a powerful and intended effect on at least some of its hearers.

## CHAPTER FIVE
# THE PREACHER AND HIS PEOPLE

MARSDEN'S SERMONS PROVIDE a rich cache of primary documentation from the early colony of New South Wales, amounting to almost five hundred thousand words. The sermons are not only a valuable resource in understanding Marsden's preaching but also the man himself, his character and his motivations. We can also glean from them some further understanding of the colony and its people as Marsden referred in his preaching to various events and happenings within the colony at the time. This includes subjects such as the gallows, the execution of innocent men, marriage and adultery, magistrates, the Aboriginals, prostitution, drunkenness, gambling, extortion, Sabbath observance and Christian charity.

Marsden lived in the colony through times of change from a penal colony to an increasingly free society. It is clear in the collections of sermons that he preached to audiences of convicts and of free settlers. His later sermons reflect the more settled times where he calls on his congregations for benevolent action. His earlier sermons indicate his struggle against immoral and illegal behaviours of those living in a penal colony.

The issues that Marsden constantly dealt with in his sermons were, on the surface, moral ones. In Sermon 4:3 Marsden says:

many of us have lived in the open and avowed violation of his laws. In Sabbath breaking, in profanation of God's name, in theft, in adultery, in drunkenness and every vice that would render us obnoxious to an holy God.

Yet the focus of Marsden's concern was not morality and social reform but salvation. This is clear in the above quotation. In it Marsden has said that these behaviours "render us obnoxious to an holy God". His focus on moral behaviour was not to encourage people to be upright citizens, even though he would have loved to see such an occurrence. Yet in his preaching Marsden addressed moral behaviour as an indication of a person's spiritual state and urged his congregations to be reconciled with God. Reconciliation with God, he believed, would result in moral behaviour and produce social change.

Sabbath breaking and profanation of God's name were activities in the colony that were of particular concern to the chaplains. Marsden's first sermon in New South Wales is reported by Marsden's biographer, J. B. Marsden, to have been on the topic of Sabbath Breaking.[44]

A notorious incident concerning Simon Burn provides a vignette of the dilemma in which the chaplain found himself with regard to both drunkenness and Sabbath breaking.[45] Burn

---

44  Marsden. *Memoirs*. p. 10
45  It seems that in the colony these two sins often went hand in hand. When the convicts were not required to work on Sundays they often spent their time in drunkenness and therefore were in no fit state to attend Divine Service. Note Marsden's words in Sermon 7:26, 'God's Sabbaths afford no rest to you from sin. Nay you probably commit greater sins on this day than you do on all the other days of the week.'

spent a considerable amount of his time in a state of inebriation. This particular incident involved Captain John Macarthur, the commanding officer in Parramatta at the time, and ultimately left Marsden and Macarthur at enmity for many years. Marsden was so incensed by Macarthur's attitude and inaction that he felt compelled to make an official complaint to the Governor. In the letter of complaint Marsden detailed the behaviour of Burn. Burn had approached the preacher one morning after divine service and in Marsden's words, "insulted me in the most daring manner".[46] Marsden believed Burn to be drunk at the time and turned to the head constable, who was present, insisting that Burn be arrested and taken before Macarthur. To the parson's dismay, Macarthur thought the complaint vexatious and dismissed Burn in his state of intoxication despite Marsden's allegations that Burn's behaviour had been riotous all that day.

For Marsden, Burn's intoxication on the Sabbath and consequent neglect of attending the Lord's House put Burn's soul, and those of others who behaved in a similar manner, of whom there was no shortage in the infant colony, at risk of eternal damnation. That Macarthur, a person of rank in the colony, should dismiss Burn along with Marsden's complaint, was clear indication in Marsden's mind, that good government and true religion were a thing far from the colony. As a minister of the Church of England, Marsden regularly led his congregation in prayer for good government and true religion,[47] but in the colony of New South Wales he would have to continue to work hard and long and at every level to see this prayer answered.

---

46  A. T. Yarwood. *Marsden of Parramatta*. Kenthurst, N.S.W.: Kangaroo Press, 1986. p.21
47  *Book of Common Prayer*. Holy Communion. Prayer for the Church Militant.

Macarthur may well have considered Burn's behaviour a bit of harmless frivolity. Seeing drunken convicts in the street on a Sunday when they were not required to work was a common occurrence. Marsden, on the other hand, believed that "To neglect God's Sabbaths is a great sin" and that those who made "God's day a day of pleasure and riot and dissipation" did so "to the great guilt and condemnation of your souls" (Sermon 7:26-27).

Marsden's concern was not for what he termed "scanty morality", but for the salvation of souls. This controversy in dealing with Burn's drunken behaviour on a Sunday and Macarthur's dismissal of the complaint highlights Marsden's character. His statements in his sermons indicate that he had not taken personal affront at Burn's behaviour (though his reaction to Macarthur may be a different matter) but his concern was the salvation of the man's soul.

In Burn's case it was his drunkenness that led him to break the Sabbath and abuse the chaplain. And yet it must be emphasised that in addressing moral issues Marsden never simply called upon his congregations to, "stop it!" His call was always to be cleansed in the blood of Christ. While he stated clearly and unequivocally that, "It is not to preach a scanty morality that we are called", he continued, "but to publish the glad tidings of a free and full salvation to a lost world, to sinners of all characters, a salvation founded in the blood of Christ purchased by the price of that blood".[48]

Marsden was not interested in "scanty morality". He did not simply want people to become "respectable" in moral behaviour. He saw immorality as an indication that people ignored the claims of Christ on their lives.

Marsden did not want to see people cut off by death in a state of

---

48  Sermon 93:12

drunkenness, because he believed that this would lead to eternal damnation. Burn suffered this very fate of dying in a drunken stupor only weeks after his encounter with Marsden. Marsden had seen it happen too often. "O ye drunkards, what if God should in the midst of one of your drunken fits arrest you by death, as he has many amongst us" (31:5).

The statement also highlights the fact that Marsden knew his various roles well. In preaching, he was the pastor who cared that his flock should know that the remedy to sin was not the avoidance of moral imperfections but a trust in the shed blood of Jesus which paid the price of that sin. While, as a magistrate, he may have earned the epithet "Flogging Parson", his sermons do not show the same apparent glee for flogging that his magisterial role indicates. In his preaching Marsden was simply the Parson who demonstrated a pastoral concern for his people. Marsden was able to compartmentalise his various roles. As the Parson he exhibited all the traits of the compassionate pastor who, as his ordination vows reminded him, had the "Cure of Souls", whereas as the Magistrate, he was able to bring the harshest punishments to bear on the bodies of the guilty (and in some cases the not guilty) in the form of the cat of nine tails.

While mostly Marsden pointed to the common sins of the inhabitants of the colony in the hope that they would view them with respect to the consequences for their eternal destiny, in Sermon 97:14 he warned that certain behaviours would also bring the judgement of civil authority:

> Many of you are guilty of uttering the most diabolical speeches in the most open and public manner, such as decency forbids me to mention in this place. Let your own consciences point them out to you. Your conduct in this

respect not only calls upon me as a minister to warn you but also upon the civil the civil (sic) power to exercise its authority to restrain your licentious and obscene speeches.

This is the only sermon in which Marsden brings together, in such close juxtaposition, the roles of the minister and of the civil power, seeing both to have a responsibility to curb immoral behaviour. This does not negate his understanding of the different purposes of the two roles. As a minister he saw the first priority was the salvation of his people and as a magistrate his role was to bring order to society.

In his preaching Marsden highlighted compassion for his people by emphasising the need to trust in the shed blood of Jesus to cleanse from sin. Marsden may have had a reputation as a harsh magistrate and come under censure for neglecting the duties of his "parish" for more worldly pursuits, but it is clear from his preaching that he took his role as pastor seriously.

The bulk of the content of Marsden's preaching shows that his concern was the spiritual wellbeing of the members of his congregation. He wanted them not to be punished for their sins in eternity but to turn from them and trust in the One who has taken the punishment for them.

## The Exclusives

Marsden was a member of a group of people in the colony who came to be known by the pejorative title, *The Exclusives*. He believed in ranks and order in society and was particularly reticent to see emancipists being accepted into the "higher ranks". His objection to sitting as Commissioner on the turnpike road with Lord and Thompson, noted in chapter four, is indicative of his exclusivist views.

While Marsden's stance against working in an official capacity with men who were living in *de facto* relationships can be understood, Macquarie's inconsistency on this matter is a little harder to comprehend. Having arrived in the colony to discover how prevalent was the practice of men and women living together without the sanction of marriage, he issued a decree condemning the practice. We can only guess at Macquarie's reasons for appointing Lord and Thompson to an official position whose living arrangements he had labelled as "scandalous and pernicious".

Not wanting to be associated with emancipists in an official position speaks clearly of Marsden's attitude towards the ranks and orders within society. This attitude marks him as a member of *The Exclusives*. It is an attitude to the ordering of society that Marsden derived from his understanding of how heaven is ordered. In Sermon 23:3 he says, "Even in heaven he has established different rank and orders amongst the angels". Not only does this order exist in heaven amongst the angels, God has directed that it also be followed on earth: "on earth also he has seen fit, that a similar order should be maintained".

Marsden believed that while these ranks and orders may exist both in heaven and on earth all people are treated equally when it comes to salvation: "the Lord will reward every man according to his works, of what rank he may be in society whether learned or ignorant". (19:8) He also called on his congregation to consider what an exalted rank, above the angels, they will have in heaven: "Consider the dignity of your character, the rank you hold in heaven and to what an inheritance you are heir to". (28:25, 27)[49]

Marsden believed these orders and ranks were appropriate on

---

49 Page 26 of this sermon is blank.

earth for good government. He declared that even from the first, one person was appointed to rule the other: "Adam should rule and that Eve should obey". Since then God has appointed parents as "the natural governors of their children" and societies "had their respective governors, some in one way, and some in another" (23:3-4).

It must be noted that Marsden held that these ranks and orders on earth were not for repression and subjugation. Those of privileged rank or authority must treat others with compassion. He believed that the way we treat our fellow human beings will be a particular focus on the day of judgement.[50] He demonstrated Christian compassion for those whom he regarded as being of the "lower ranks" by calling upon those with means to support the people living in the Benevolent Asylum:

> Many of them have a just claim to your benevolence, who have spent their time and strength in your service or in improving the general welfare of the community. They have laboured and we have entered into their labours. They have contributed to build our houses, to clear our lands, (to) plant our vineyards, to feed our flocks and herds, and to raise our bread, and to add to our comfort, (prosperity) and safety. They have made highways for us thro the wilderness. Now their natural strength is exhausted, by age, toils, sickness, and numerous infirmities on account of which they claim, and justly, our benevolence and compassion. (66:23)

---

50 Sermon 66:2-3. In speaking of what will happen on judgment day Marsden says, 'That the whole of our principles and conduct will be taken into consideration, there can be no doubt, but there is one point that will be inquired into, and will be regarded as a certain evidence of all the rest, viz., our activity in doing good to our fellow creatures for Christ's sake.'

Marsden has been described by some as a vindictive, petulant, even psychopathic personality. A contemporary, W. C. Wentworth, described him as, "a reverend hypocrite; a crafty, turbulent, and ambitious priest; a man of the most rancorous and vindictive spirit".[51] Sermon 66 gives a different insight into the man. In this sermon Marsden has expressed a clear understanding of how he and others have benefitted from the labours of others. He speaks about his concern for those who have laboured for the "general welfare of the community" and he has the belief that they "have a just claim on our benevolence". With these words we see in Marsden a person who is genuinely thankful for the work these people have done and we see a compassion for them who are now spent and in need of care in their old age and infirmity.

In a context of an evangelical heritage M. A. Roberts speaks of a "moral reform tradition" in which he believes the middle class evangelicals developed a sense of obligation "aroused by unease about the moral consequences of material advance".[52] It may be that in this tradition of voluntarism Marsden was supporting, and encouraging others to support, the Benevolent Asylum because of some unease about the moral consequences of his own increased wealth. Despite this unease and an expression of concern for the welfare of people who had laboured hard for him and for others,

---

51 Charles White. *Early Australian History. Convict Life in New South Wales and Van Diemen's Land*. Bathurst. Free Press, 1889. Reproduced by Forgotten Books. 2013. p. 217.

52 M. J. D. Roberts. *Making English morals: voluntary association and moral reform in England, 1787–1886*. Cambridge. Cambridge University Press. 2004. p. viii. On the issue of what might have been motivating evangelicals to form voluntary societies Roberts further says, 'By means of volunteer associational action they created and successfully transmitted across several generations a collective memory of cultural heritage and obligation, as well as a commitment to a form of public action self-consciously presented as aiming to transcend individual or sectional self-interest.' p. viii.

Marsden's views on the ordering of society were in line with *The Exclusives*. It is right that he be included in their ranks for the attitudes he expressed towards emancipists in particular. He believed that God had so ordered societies around the world with those who rule and those who obey.

## The Gallows, Innocent Men and Women of Shame

Marsden did not preach on topical issues and he referred to very few subjects from contemporary colonial life to illustrate his sermons. This means there is not a great deal of content in the sermons about incidents in the colony, though they are not entirely bereft of references. Through these we are able to gain a glimpse of the preacher's perspective on colonial life at this time.

Two specific activities Marsden addresses in Sermon 4:3 are theft and adultery. It is interesting to note that these two activities often went hand in hand in the colony. Marsden was not the only person of rank in New South Wales to note that illegitimate liaisons often led men and women into crime and eventually to suffer the full weight of the law. Governor Hunter was one who lamented the fate of fine soldiers who were eventually brought to the gallows having been found guilty of theft resulting, he believed, from their desire to please their mistresses.

In Sermon 13:14 Marsden has written down the side of the page a comment that gives rise to the possibility he thought some who had been executed in the colony had been innocent men. In the last paragraph of this page Marsden speaks of the injustice Jesus suffered at his trial and says that even the betraying Judas declared Jesus innocent. He then makes the point that the laws under which they now live would not permit such a miscarriage of justice, and yet, down the side of the page he has written the comment, "There are instances amongst ourselves where men have been condemned". In the context of this sermon it is clear that Marsden meant that he thought within the colony *innocent* men have been condemned.

The period between 1826 and 1837 has been described as, "the heyday of capital punishment" in New South Wales where "377 prisoners were hanged".[53] G. D. Woods writes, "As to early punitive savagery, the sheer number of executions was staggering".[54] In another article Castle says, "One of the bloodiest periods for public execution in New South Wales occurred under Governors Darling and Bourke from 1826 to 1836, with 363 executions taking place".[55] In this environment, of itself, there is nothing surprising about Marsden's comment written down the side of a page of this sermon. It seems, however, from the context of his sermon, Marsden is referring to innocent men being hanged. In speaking of the innocence of Jesus, who was yet condemned, it is likely Marsden means "innocent men" in the colony have been condemned, even though he has stated in the body of the sermon that under British law such a miscarriage of justice would not be permitted.

Marsden also believed that, despite the superiority of British law, perjury led to the condemnation of innocent people. In Sermon 91:4 in speaking on the issue of perjury he says:

It is a crime that has risen to the most dreadful heights

---

[53] Tim Castle, "Constructing Death: Newspaper Reports of Executions in Colonial New South Wales, 1826–1837", *Journal of Australian Colonial History* 9, no. 2007 (2007). p.51.

[54] G. D. Woods, "A History of Criminal Law in New South Wales the Colonial Period, 1788–1900", ed. Mark Findlay Chris Cunneen, Julie Stubbs, *Sydney Institute of Criminology Monograph Series No 17*. Sydney: The Federation Press, 2002. p.1.

[55] Tim Castle, "Watching Them Hang. Capital Punishment and Public Support in Colonial New South Wales, 1826–1836", *History Australia* 5, no. 2 (2008).

amongst ourselves and instances are not wanting in this Colony where the innocent have been condemned and executed on the evidence of perjured persons.

In Sermon 91 when preaching about Jezebel's use of corrupt magistrates against Naboth, Marsden again comments on the superiority of the British legal system:

it would hardly be possible under British laws to induce the magistrates and judges to join in a conspiracy to cut off the life of an innocent person. (91:6)

If it was Marsden's belief that innocent men had suffered execution, he was not alone in it. Other chaplains in the colony took action when they believed in the innocence of a man who found himself at the end of a hangman's rope. The execution of Thomas Lynch is reported in the *Sydney Gazette*, 13 January 1829. Both J. D. Lang and Father Power believed Lynch to be innocent and made last minute attempts at a temporary stay of execution.[56] It seems that despite Marsden's observation in his sermon of the superiority of British law, executions of innocent people could and did happen in the colony.

While the intervention of the clergy in the execution of Thomas Lynch may have been a rare and even isolated incident, it is clear from his preaching Marsden believed that a man could be brought to the gallows from what, initially, would be seen by many as the most trivial of reasons. He states quite clearly on several occasions his opposition to idleness. He extends this in Sermon 76:22 to a belief that idleness leads to the gallows. He says,

---

56  Castle. "Constructing Death". p.60.

> If men would only use moderate industry, none would
> be brought to the gallos (sic) here for breaking this
> commandment. How wretched depraved & corrupted are the
> minds of those men who rather chose to withdraw themselves
> from all civil society than eat the bread of honest industry.

But it is not idleness alone that will bring a man to the gallows. It is the company men keep that will see them strangled in the hangman's noose. In Sermon 7:24 Marsden says,

> Few ... come to the gallos (sic), but who are led there by
> some infamous strumpet. Alas for these men. They see
> their sin and folly in their punishment, often too late for
> reformation. Let me entreat you as Moses did the Israelites
> to refrain from the tents of these wicked women. Avoid
> their company and society as you would avoid hell. Let them
> wander unnoticed as vagabonds & outcasts from society till a
> sense of sin and shame bring them to repentance & reform.

Marsden has some support from Grace Karskens for this wariness of convict women, and their ability to lure men to their ruin. Karskens writes, "Men in authority were wary of convict women too, because of their power to seduce soldiers away from their duty and sailors from their ships".[57] She goes on to quote Hunter[58] who blamed the company of convict women for the downfall of six marines, "the flower of our battalion". The six, James Baker, James Brown, Richard Dukes, Thomas Jones, Luke Haynes and Richard Askew, were hanged in March 1789 for robbing the stores.

---

57  Grace Karskens. *The Colony: A History of Early Sydney*. Sydney. Allen & Unwin. 2009. p.318.
58  John Hunter. *An Historical Journal*. London. 1793. p. 94.

To be fair, Karskens believes this attitude to the convict women left a long legacy, which ignored the "women who were householders, workers, business- and tradeswomen, mothers and makers of community in early Sydney".[59] Perhaps Marsden contributed to this ignorance. Certainly this sermon shows that he believed good men were being led astray by "abandoned" women. There is no sermon in the collection that shows Marsden's praise for women who were "makers of community in early Sydney". And yet Marsden is not a one-eyed misogynist. It was not just the women who led the men astray. In Sermon 61:13-14 Marsden lamented the total disregard of the injuries licentious men do to hundreds of women in the colony:

> How many hundreds of unfortunate women are there in these settlements who may date the origin of their disgrace, their banishment and their sufferings to the arts and designs of abandoned (vicious) libertines, who are totally regardless of the injuries they do by their licencious *(sic)* passions.

## Marriage and Adultery

Marsden has come under criticism from many quarters for referring to women living in a *de-facto* relationship as "Concubines".[60] This statement in 1806 seems to have stained his reputation from then on with regard to his attitude towards the women of the colony. Babette Smith in *Australia's Birthstain* writes that Marsden's "campaign to reform the morals of the women convicts in particular

---

59 Karskens. *The Colony.* p.321.
60 'Statement of the married and unmarried women and the number of their children in NSW, 1806'. *Essays 1806.* ML. M 18

played a significant role in creating their bad reputation".[61] Smith does acknowledge that there were others who had similar views to Marsden and quotes:

> the now infamous passage where Lieutenant Ralph Clark described his reaction at Botany Bay of the sight of more female convicts arriving on the *Lady Juliana* in 1790. "No, no – surely not! My God – not more of those damned whores. Never have I known worse women".[62]

Annette Salt, in *These Outcast Women*, referring to the Female Factory at Parramatta acknowledges that the:

> Factory became the means of socially controlling ... women. It could control their promiscuity by providing the means and incentive for contracting sanctified marriages. It could control the deployment of labour, and provide productive and profitable employment for convicted women.[63]

Salt then shows that Marsden's description and others like it, was not uncommon. She names Patrick Colquhoun,[64] T W Plumber,[65] and William Henry[66] as men who had described these women

---

61 Babette Smith. *Australia's Birthstain: The Startling Legacy of the Convict Era.* Crows Nest, N.S.W. Allen & Unwin. 2008. pp. 206-207.
62 Smith. *Australia's Birthstain.* p. 207. Ref: Ralph Clark. 'The Letter Book'. ML. Call Number: MLMSS 3429
63 Annette Salt. *These Outcast Women: The Parramatta Female Factory 1821–1848.* Macquarie Colonial Papers. Sydney. Hale & Iremonger. 1984. p. 120.
64 Salt. *These Outcast Women.* p. 26. Ref: Thompson, E. P., *The Making of the English Working Class.* Harmondsworth, 1977. p.60.
65 Salt. *These Outcast Women.* p. 35. Ref: T W Plumber to Macquarie 4 May 1809. HRNSW, 7. Sydney, 1901. p.120.
66 Salt. *These Outcast Women.* p. 38. Ref: Wm. Henry to LMS. 29 Aug 1799, HRNSW 3. p.715.

as "prostitutes". She also names "George Sutter, a settler, [who] contrasted convict women with "virtuous women" as though the two terms were mutually exclusive".[67]

Marsden was also not alone in wanting to see women married so that the moral behaviour in the colony might be raised. Salt points to the fact that "surgeon Cunningham advocated that female convicts be speedily married, as the resultant responsibility would make them industrious, offset male depravity and increase the population".[68] Salt also notes that "The *Sydney Gazette* advocated marriage and parenthood as 'the greatest inspiration to reform and industry in female convicts'".[69] The imbalance in the sexes and the lack of adequate accommodation gave rise to a high level of immorality in the colony which was remarked on by numbers of people who sought solutions to the problem. Marsden was among them, but alone singled out for criticism for his description of the women caught up in this system.

When he first arrived in the colony, Governor Lachlan Macquarie noticed immediately that *de facto* relationships were common practice and decreed that men and women should regularise their cohabitation by entering into marriage. Marsden was not averse to mentioning this particular issue in his preaching. In Sermon 88:20-21 he says,

> How many (married) men and women are there amongst us who have forsaken their own husbands and wives and

---

67 Salt. *These Outcast Women*. p. 38. Ref: Suttor to Bligh. 10 Feb 1809. HRNSW p.23.
68 Salt. *These Outcast Women*. p. 42. Ref: Peter Cunningham. *Two Years in NSW*, London, 1827, p.323.
69 Salt. *These Outcast Women*. p. 80. Ref: SG 'Report on the Female Factory' 24 June 1826

gone after others, and are at this moment living with them. Tho these men (married) and women did faithfully promise before God the angels and their fellow creatures in the most solemn and religious manner in the name of the Father and of the Son and of the Holy Ghost that they never would be guilty of this offence. And yet they are living in the habitual commission of adultry *(sic)* not withstanding their solemn vows and promises. Surely these people can never believe that their *(sic)* is a God that taketh vengeance. If they did they would sooner suffer strangling and death than act in this very way. (88:20-21)

The issue was not simply that men and women were living in *de facto* relationships but that many of them had left wives and husbands back in England and had taken up temporary cohabitation in the colony. Further, their living together in the colony was producing offspring. Once a man had served his time and wished to return to England these children and their mothers were abandoned as the man returned to his legal spouse and their legitimate children. Ultimately, it is the spiritual condition and prospects of people that Marsden was concerned about in these comments. If people who "are living in the habitual commission of adultery" believed that there is a God who will take vengeance, they would prefer "strangling and death" rather than to continue in their adulterous relationships.

While Marsden may have preached against this immorality and Macquarie may have stated his opposition, neither approach appears to have had much success in raising the moral standard of the colony. Marsden declared this to be the case. While he may have made his efforts at improving colonial morality both from the pulpit and the bench, Sermon 68:9 gives an insight into how the magistrate and preacher ultimately viewed these efforts:

We see (daily) that nothing can alter the dispositions and conduct of wicked men, that all calls from heaven, and all punishments from men are ineffectual.[70]

70 Despite not being able to stop the practice Marsden did show some compassion and understanding on December 27, 1820 when he gave evidence to the Bigge Commission concerning two touching cases. He was asked, "Have you frequently discovered that women who are married here after their arrival, had husbands in England and that those husbands join them here after their second marriage?" He responded, "I have seen several instances of this kind, and one very affecting instance in a person named Patrick Emmentter, who lived at Parramatta. He married a prisoner here, a young women woman of two or three and twenty and they seemed to be very happy. Walking down the street one evening with her husband she came up to me and in great agitation said, 'My first husband is come Sir, & is now at the Derwent.' She was so distressed she did not know what to do, her first husband had gone on board a man of war and she thought he had been dead. I told her she did very wrong not to inform me that she was married and that she deserved to be severely punished. In a short time her first husband arrived & they all three, the 1st & 2nd husband & the wife came to my house. She said that her 2nd husband had been a kind and good husband to her, & he said that she had been a good wife & lived happily together. They were all three greatly affected. I said to the woman you now have 2 husbands, with which do you think you can be the most happy. She said I have been very happy with the 2nd husband but if I could have my choice I would take the first. I told her she had done very wrong, but that as the 1st husband had a legal claim upon her she must adopt him. The 2nd husband was much affected, & indeed they all were, and she left Parramatta that evening with the 1st husband. The 2nd husband had been very unhappy ever since. I remember also a man named John Jennings, who was a Chief Constable at Parramatta and succeeded G. Barrington. He called upon me one day and told me that his lawful wife had arrived at Sydney & wished that I could advise him what step to take, as he had 2 children by the women with whom he was then cohabiting. He was greatly distressed, & I told him that he would be obliged to receive his wife tho he said that he had been separated from her for 9 years. He could not muster resolution to go to Sydney and see his wife but she at length arrived at Parramatta and after learning where he lived knocked at the door & asked whether John Jennings lived there. The woman with whom he lived having heard something of it, said that no John Jennings lived there. Jennings was in the next room and called out before he saw her, 'Fanny I am here'. They met, & in great distress of mind he furnished the other woman with means to live and return home and she went to England to her friends. On my arrival there I enquired after her, & I was informed that she had been hung for some crime that she had committed. Jennings himself died of a broken heart very soon after the woman quitted him". Marsden's evidence to Bigge, 27 December, 1820.

If Marsden thought both his efforts as a preacher and as a magistrate were ineffectual, why did he persevere, or why did he not look for some other strategy? Some believe he just gave up the struggle and turned his focus elsewhere. According to Governor Brisbane, he gave his energies more to indulgence "in private trade".[71] Likewise, a modern-day historian writes that Marsden saw his vindication from God came not from his efforts as a clergyman or a magistrate but from "the prosperity of his labours". She says Marsden's prosperity, "was a sign of divine vindication [and] was at the heart of Marsden's self-understanding".[72]

A closer look at what motivated Marsden as he preached shows that both the contemporary commentator and the modern-day historian have not understood the man. His sermons show that Marsden had a genuine desire to see men and women converted to Christ and he gave his energy and passions to seeing this happen as he preached each Sunday. He believed if a change were to come about in a person, it would be by the movement of God's Spirit in their lives. It would not depend on the cajoling words of a preacher alone, nor the sentence passed by a magistrate. As Marsden wrote to Mrs Stokes after having been in the colony for just two years, "There has not been any shaking yet among the dry bones, but the Son of Man is commanded to prophecy and I hope by and by the Lord will command the wind to blow. Stir up thy strength O God & come amongst us".[73]

---

71   J. D. Heydon. 'Brisbane, Sir Thomas Makdougall (1773 – 1860)', *Australian Dictionary of Biography*, Volume 1, Melbourne University Press. 1966. pp 151-155.
72   Meredith Lake, "Samuel Marsden, Work and the Limits of Evangelical Humanitarianism", *History Australia* Vol 7, no. 3 (2010). p.57.8
73   George Mackaness. (Ed.) *Some Private Correspondence of the Rev Samuel Marsden and Family 1794–1824*. Sydney. Mackaness. 1942. p. 17.

The reference to the shaking of the dry bones is a reference to Ezekiel 37 where the Spirit of God comes upon a valley of dry bones and gives them the breath of life so that they become the people of God. Clearly Marsden believed this movement of the Spirit of God was necessary to move people into life. He also believed it was his task to call upon people to take up life whilst, once he had done this duty, the responsibility lay back on the hearers themselves to respond:

> I am commanded to warn every man, to entreat every man, to exhort every man to turn to God and live. (46:22)

> It is my duty to warn you, to exhort you, and to beseech you to turn to God and live. But when I have done this I am clear from your blood. Your sin will then be found upon your own heads. (68:19)

In Sermon 6:3 he makes it clear that, without the Spirit of God, people only have a "relish for sensual gratifications", but if they are "born again of the Spirit" they will have "experienced a divine change to have passed upon their souls". What Marsden is in fact saying is that only by this "divine change" would there be any change in the morality of colonial life. If he had been consistent in this theological position he may well have declined the role of Magistrate.

## On Magistrates and the rule of law

Marsden saw his duty as a preacher was to be an obedient proclaimer of the things of God. If he did his job, the Holy Spirit would follow with His work of changing the hearts of men and women. Marsden's preaching also gives an insight into the duties and responsibilities of the role of Magistrate as he saw it. Sermon 56 deals specifically with the issue of magistrates. Marsden writes:

> magistrates as well as all in authority are bound by every civil moral and religious obligation to punish evil doers – they do not bear the sword of justice in vain. (56:5)

The magistrate is simply bound to "punish evil doers". And so, "The institution of magistrates and judges is a necessary part of every well-ordered government" (56:4). "Indeed without such an institution the laws themselves would be altogether vain and useless" (56:5). On this view magistrates are functionaries of the law which they simply administer. The law stands on its own for the good government of society: "men must be kept within the bounds of established laws which are enacted for the general good" (56:5).

While Marsden believed that his roles as preacher and magistrate were not trying to achieve the same ends, he nuanced this view with an understanding that preachers and magistrates did not have mutually exclusive roles. The duties of the preacher included the duty to "put them (the professors of Christianity) in mind to be subject to principalities and powers, and to obey magistrates" (23:1-2). "The office of ministers is to preach the gospel of Christ". At the same time they must not overlook the duty that the gospel of Christ puts on the people "as members of civil communion" (23:1).

In Marsden's view, God had placed magistrates and governors in a civil society to "do all in their power for the suppression of iniquity" (23:4). The "civil magistrate is a minister to the[m] for good, a revenger to execute wrath upon him that doeth evil" (27:1). Further, Marsden believed that magistrates were to use their influence for "the maintenance of piety in the world ... and are therefore called his ministers" (63:3-4). These views on the roles of magistrates and governors in the ordering of society for suppression of iniquity and maintenance of piety, gesture towards an evangelical understanding of mission. This is not that Marsden thought that a well ordered society was the way to do Christian mission but rather that a well ordered society created a safe place in which to do mission. This idea may explain Marsden's understanding when he accepted the role of a magistrate. He was not trying to convert people with the lash, but rather he expected a well ordered, and therefore safe society, was the best place to do mission. As a magistrate he could help create a safe place. As a preacher he could then proclaim the gospel to a people who inhabited a safe place.

Marsden also believed there was a distinction between Christian forgiveness and the penalty of law:

> Christian forgiveness does not interfere with human laws. It does not forbid governors and magistrates to execute them since they are appointed of God on purpose to enforce them. (89:4)

Because governors and magistrates are "appointed of God" it is appropriate for the punishment of the law to be carried out, taking precedence over Christian forgiveness.

While it is plain that Marsden saw the roles of preacher and magistrate as distinct but complementary, Quinn misses the point when he comments that Marsden "was soon convinced of the greater efficacy of the lash".[74] Quinn's thesis is that Marsden thought he might have greater success in converting people through

---

74  Richard Quinn. *Samuel Marsden: Altar Ego*. Wellington. Dunmore Publishing Ltd. 2008. p.56.

his role as a magistrate where he was not able to as a preacher. In Sermon 97:6 Marsden answers this accusation long before it is made: "Outward restraints are good, but can avail but little towards inward conversion". He knew that "inward conversion" is the work of the Holy Spirit. He did not believe he could persuade anyone to true religion by ordering a flogging. Any "divine change" in a person's life came from being "born again of the Holy Spirit" (6:4). A person could not even approach God unless drawn by the Holy Spirit: "We have no will to approach unto him unless the Holy Spirit incline our hearts" (95:4). The work of conversion was the work of the Holy Spirit. The work of the preacher was to preach. The work of the magistrate was the appointment of God for the good government of society which created a "safe place" in which the gospel could then be preached. Punishments meted out from the bench, however, would not be tempered by Christian forgiveness.

While Marsden constantly called on his congregations to resist sin and turn away from all immoral behaviour, he recognised a person could only do this in the power of the Holy Spirit:

> St. Paul tells us that he resisted sin and strove against it … This however cannot be done effectively but by the assistance of the Holy Spirit … all our help must come from God. To attempt this work without calling upon God for the gracious aid of his Holy Spirit will be in vain. (43:10)

## The Natives of this Colony

In the entire Moore College collection of 98 sermons there are just two where Marsden makes a reference to Australian Aboriginal people. These references say nothing of the state of the people nor express a hope of their improvement or conversion. In the first reference which comes from Sermon 10:15 Marsden says:

> We need not go amongst the untutored Africans or Indians, or the natives of this colony to be made sensible that mankind have lost all fear and reverence for a supreme being, but even we who have been born in a Christian country and blessed with the knowledge of divine revelation, give the fullest demonstration of our enmity against God, and manifest this enmity by our wicked works.

This is a telling comment about how Marsden saw the spiritual state of the colonisers. In his view it is to be expected that the "untutored Africans or Indians or the natives of this colony" would have no fear or reverence for God because they have not heard of the Christian God. But Marsden's focus is on the behaviour of the colonists. Having "been born in a Christian country and blessed with the knowledge of divine revelation" it may be expected that their behaviour would reflect that knowledge. Marsden's point, though, is that even with this knowledge, there is no behavioural change which would show evidence of this knowledge of God. Rather there continues to be "enmity by our wicked works".

This is the call of the preacher for consistent behaviour. This is the call of the preacher to reflect on the fact that having heard of the Christian God, the hearers must consider what changes should take place in their living. Marsden again demonstrates his pastoral focus in his inclusive language. He is not blasting his congregation for *their* behaviour but he speaks of "*our* wicked works". The preacher identifies with his congregation. Ultimately Marsden is speaking of an inconsistent Christian living and he is calling on his people to respond to the message they have been privileged to hear; to show that they have understood the gospel message by changed behaviour in life.

This reference to the Aboriginal people is also of interest because of Marsden's well known critical comments against them. Marsden is on record as saying that the Australian Aborigine is the most degraded of all human beings.[75] He is not, however, the only person of the time to make derogatory comments about the Australian Aboriginal. Te Pahi, the Māori chief who visited Sydney in 1805, challenged the Aboriginals for going about stark naked.[76] LMS missionaries who had fled to Sydney from Tahiti also made adverse comparisons between the Australian Aboriginal and other South Sea Islanders.[77] The comments in this sermon are not so much critical as a statement of fact as Marsden sees it. He refers to several people groups who have no knowledge of the Christian God and holds them up to his congregation as an example, pointing out that they, who have been "blessed with the knowledge of divine

---

75  Marsden to Pratt, Secretary to the CMS, 24 February 1819, in John Rawson Elder, *The Letters and Journals of Samuel Marsden 1765–1838*. Dunedin: Sidney Kiek & Son, 1932. pp. 231-2.

76  Rachel Standfield. *Race and Identity in the Tasman World, 1769-1840*. London. Pickering & Chatto. 2012. Kindle edition: Location 87.

77  See Marsden's letter to the Rev Josiah Pratt, 24 February 1819, quoted in Elder, 1932, p. 231. On others making disparaging comments on the Australian Aboriginal and other native peoples see: "Religious News" *Montreal Daily Witness* April 4. 1868 which reports on the Moravian mission, 'to those most degraded of all human beings, the inhabitants of the interior of Australia.' http://news.google.com/newspapers?nid=33&dat= 18680404&id=QNYdAAAAIBAJ&sjid=nh8DAAAAIBAJ&pg=1952,4419169 Accessed 26 Dec. 2013. Willets, Jacob. *A Geography for the Use of Schools*. Potter. 1831. 'The Hottentots are described as some of the most degraded of all human beings' p.112. Digitised by Google. http://books.google.com.au/books?id=5AEWAAAAYAAJ &pg=PA112&lpg=PA112&dq=%22 Accessed 26 Dec. 2013. See also: Anne O'Brien, 'Kitchen Fragments and Garden Stuff: Poor Law Discourse and Indigenous People in early colonial New South Wales', *Australian Historical Studies* 39 (2008), p.152.

revelation", should have a greater demonstration in their lives of godly Christian behaviour.

In the second reference to Aboriginal people in the Moore College collection the "natives of this Colony" are again held up to the congregation as examples of people who are ignorant of God:

> Many here would not be men of such wicked and abandoned characters if they had no more knowledge of men and things, no more knowledge of the supreme being than the ignorant natives of this Colony. (81:10)

As much as the natives might be ignorant of the things of God, Marsden is saying to his congregation that if they had as much knowledge as the natives of the things of God, they would demonstrate that knowledge with better behaviour than they now have. These comments place a different perspective and context on Marsden's words that the natives of the colony were the "most degraded" of all human beings. The comments in this sermon are an acknowledgement by Marsden that the Aboriginal is morally superior to the convict.

Another reference to "natives" in Sermon 34:23-24 is a more generic reference. The reference is to "natives" in general rather than "the natives of this Colony" in particular. In this sermon Marsden uses them as an example to his congregation of those who are responding to the gospel and who will be in heaven while members of the congregation who are not responding to the good news proclaimed to them will be barred from entrance:

> What anguish, what despair, what agony, what weeping, what wailing, what gnashing of teeth will seize your souls when you shall see the natives of the south sea islands, with

other heathen natives sitting in the kingdom of God and ye yourselves thrust out.

These few references to Aboriginal people in the Moore College collection of Marsden's surviving sermons indicate several things about Marsden's understanding of the "native people of the Colony". First, we again see that Marsden does not use his time in the pulpit to deliberate on controversial issues. He does not try to justify himself against the criticisms of Campbell, that he was more interested in being the "Mohamed of the South Seas", than caring about the Aboriginal people of the colony.[78] He is consistent in the demarcation of his roles and here is faithful to the task of the preacher. His sermons, showing his pastoral heart by his inclusive language, constantly call upon his hearers to examine themselves and to be cleansed by the blood of Jesus. He does not muddy the waters with political issues.

---

78 In a letter under the nom de plume of *Philo Free*, Campbell (the Governor's Private Secretary) had written in the Gazette of 4 January 1817, accusing those involved in the South Seas mission of introducing alcohol and guns to their own financial advantage while neglecting the native population of New South Wales. Campbell defended his action to the governor in publishing the letter on the grounds that he had been indignant that Marsden had not attended a meeting of the natives at Parramatta which the governor had convened, believing that Marsden was opposed to any efforts at civilising the Aboriginals. Far from neglecting the welfare of the Australian Aboriginals, in a letter dated 25 April 1810 to the Church Missionary Society, Marsden wrote in connection with the delay of sending missionaries on to New Zealand because of fears for their safety after the massacre of the crew of the *Boyd* in New Zealand. He proposed to retain these missionaries at Parramatta and put them to work in the 'instruction of the natives of New Holland.' This proposal was to 'make some little establishment for the accommodation of our own natives, and those of the islands who may visit us.' Letter from Marsden to CMS Committee, 3 May 1810 in S. M. Johnstone. *Samuel Marsden, a Pioneer of Civilization in the South Seas*. Sydney. Angus & Robertson. 1932. p.86. See also Chapter Five Sanction and Strategy.

Secondly, his references to the "ignorant" natives are not derogatory in nature. Marsden uses the term as a simple statement of fact. Those who have not heard the gospel are ignorant of the things of God. This ignorance, however, does not place them in an inferior position. All people have equal opportunity to respond to the gospel and those "natives of the south sea islands, with other heathen natives" will be "sitting in the kingdom of God" (Sermon 34:24) because they will leave their ignorance behind and respond to the gospel when they hear it, whereas those members of Marsden's congregation who have been born in a Christian country but have not responded to the gospel, will be left out and not sitting in the Kingdom of God.

Marsden made efforts to engage with the Aboriginal people by bringing children into his household, training them as domestic servants. These efforts invariably proved unsuccessful both in seeing these children become members of a white community and in conversion to Christianity. This attitude to the Aboriginal people is well criticised but it did not mean for Marsden that he believed that Christianity was only for "civilised" people. His sermons show his belief that all people of whichever race must make their own response to the offer of salvation in Jesus Christ. If those of British descent were not responding they would see the natives of the South Seas entering heaven before them.

## Prostitution, Sobriety and Children

In calling people to more moral behaviour Marsden wanted them to reflect on their lifestyle choices primarily in the light of the account they may give to God. While he did call for social change in his sermons, as was common within the evangelical milieu, his sermons reveal more of a desire to see people making sure of a place in heaven:

> Let me exhort you who have run to the greatest excesses in iniquity to stop this day and come to some serious reflection. Had God punished you as your crimes deserved where would you now have been? I leave your consciences to answer. (Sermon 9:22)

Drunkenness and prostitution are two crimes Marsden singles out that "keep the Colony in a constant state of torment and alarm" (75:13). He believed these were the two causes of a man turning to theft, perjury and murder:

> These crimes find constant employment for the different benches of magistrates thro the Colony and our Court of Criminal Jurisdiction. They lead to every kind of robberies, (&) perjuries and murders. They bring the utmost ruin and distress upon families, destroy the prospects of the rising generation, and fill the Colony with poor distressed orphans, or children forsaken by one or both their parents. There is scarcely a week passes but but *(sic)* some man or woman falls a sacrifice to the sin of drunkenness or whoredom, with respect to drunkenness there is scarcely a street a lane a highway, or even a prison (in the Colony) in which some drunkard has not breathed his last breath in a state of intoxication. (75:14-15)

And yet Marsden is not simply concerned at the sight of people dying in the streets from intoxication and the effect that has on the general population. When he notes that "some of you who are accustomed to be intoxicated at every opportunity", his desire is to call upon his hearers to consider the consequences of this behaviour for their eternal salvation: "what do you think in your serious sober moments. Do you ever think that you shall not inherit the kingdom of God?" (88:10). In his sermons this eschatological focus is more evident than a social reform agenda for which the evangelicals were well known. Further to this Marsden says that the sight of women rolling drunk in the streets was not uncommon:

> To see women rowling *(sic)* drunk in the streets and to hear them belching out the most horrid oaths [and] curses has ever been considered as the greatest disgrace to any society. Yet is it not uncommon amongst us. Women have lost all regard for God, their sex and society & are only fit fuel for hell. (97:15)

So common had the sight of drunken people in the street become that Marsden believed the ill effect of it on the general population is not apparent:

> The Corinthians were also accused of drunkenness. And may not many of us be charged with the same beastly crime. It is become so common a practice *(sic)* amongst us that its malignity does not appear. (88:22)

But his concerns were not limited to drunkenness and prostitution. Marsden believed that every sin that people could possibly be addicted to was flagrantly practiced in the colony:

> There is scarcely a single sin which the apostle hath specified by name, and to which the heathens were addicted but what is most flagrant amongst us. (88:19)

Part of Marsden's concern in delineating the sins of the people in the colony was a desire to see them honouring God and making sure of a place for themselves in heaven. But he could see the ill effects the behaviour he opposed was having on the coming generations and spoke about the bad example being set by those who were parents:

> They bring the utmost ruin and distress upon families, destroy the prospects of the rising generation, and fill the Colony with poor distressed orphans, or children forsaken by one or both their parents. (75:14)

There are two other references in the Moore College collection of Marsden's sermons to the plight of children in the colony, Sermons 35 & 88. They are in a similar vein, speaking of children who have lost one or both parents. Marsden is likely to have also been aware of the decision of leading evangelicals in York in 1786 to establish Sunday Schools declaring them to be "necessary to the rescuing of the children of poor parents from the low habits of vice and idleness".[79] And yet in his preaching there is no call to action to promote or support any social activity in this area. Here is a notable trend in Marsden's preaching. In the colony he was active in promoting the evangelical social reform agenda, as evidenced by his involvement in education, in the establishment of the Benevolent Asylum and the women's factory at Parramatta against inaction by Governor Macquarie. However, in general, he does not promote this social agenda in his preaching by a call to action. The exception to this is Sermon 66 discussed earlier and the sermon

---

[79] J. Howard. *Historical Sketch of the Origin and work of the York Incorporated (Church of England) Sunday School Committee*. Second edition. York. 1896. p. 7. Quoted by Edward Royal. 'Evangelicals and Education.' in John Wolffe (Ed.) Evangelical Faith and Public Zeal: Evangelicals and Society in Britain 1780–1980. London. SPCK. 1995. p. 118.

following the wreck of the *Edward Lombe* where he called on his congregation in this specific incident to give to those in need. Other than these two examples Marsden's sermons serve simply to warn. He does this by pointing out unacceptable behaviour. The only call to action is a call to trust in the shed blood of Jesus. Marsden's sermons are not a vehicle of evangelical social strategy with a call to social reform.

In Sermon 81 Marsden spoke about how Abraham, Isaac and Jacob passed on the things of God to their children through "holy conversation". He tried to encourage his congregation to follow these godly examples, but says "I fear we have few Abrahams amongst us. Few that make it their study to train up their children in the way they should go" (81:14). He then asked directly if there were any such parents in the colony and answered his rhetorical question in the negative:

> Do we see any parents amongst ourselves take pains to instruct them in their duty? On the contrary they seem rather to study to corrupt their infant minds with everything that can render them obnoxious to ~~society~~ God and society, and bring themselves to shame (&) ruin. (81:15-16)

Marsden believed that most children in the colony had been corrupted by their parents' poor example but called upon those parents to cease their immorality out of pity for the children:

> There are few children here but have acquired a great degree of knowledge how to do evil. They are ripe in iniquity. You who are parents ought to abstain from many scandalous vices in which you live out of pity to your own children. Few of you would wish your children to be situated as you are or have

been. You would not wish them to be brought to that public disgrace which your vices have brought you to. (81:16)

Of note here is Marsden's assessment of the effects these crimes had on families and the colony as a whole. He believed these crimes destroyed the prospects of the rising generation and filled the colony with poor distressed orphans and forsaken children. There was scarcely any street where a drunken person did not die every week. So little value did the people of the colony in general put on human life that very little thought was given to those terrible circumstances.

Marsden's concerns alert us to the fact that these things were a common enough occurrence. They paint for us a picture of people in destitute circumstances having an adverse impact on the young people of the colony and of the general population. So common had these circumstances become, the people became indifferent to them. Of drunkenness specifically Marsden painted a bleak picture. He says in Sermon 75:14-15:

> There is scarcely a week passes but but some man or woman falls a sacrifice to the sin of drunkenness or ~~whoredom~~, with respect to drunkenness there is scarcely a street a lane a highway, ~~or even a prison~~ (in the Colony) in which some drunkard has not breathed his last breath in a state of intoxication. Yet the living lay it not to heart. These awful deaths are so common that they are thought no more of than a ~~buch~~ butcher slaughtering an ox or a sheep. So little value is put upon human life.

Licence may be allowed for the preacher's hyperbole where he says, "there is scarcely a street a lane a highway in the colony in which some drunkard has not breathed his last". And yet Marsden's lament seems more to be at the low value of human life exhibited by an apparent indifference to the loss of life. It is interesting to note that the death of Simon Burn just weeks after his encounter with Marsden was at the hand of a butcher who ran him through with a knife. Marsden may well have had Burn's death in mind as he penned these words lamenting how cheap life had become in the colony.

In Sermon 31 Marsden gives further insight into how he viewed drunkenness in the colony. His text for this sermon is 1 Peter 4:7, "The end of all things is at hand; be ye therefore sober & watch unto prayer". It is one of a number of New Year sermons in the Moore College corpus. In these Marsden speaks of how God had taken many people from their midst in the past year. He then calls on the congregation to consider that in the coming year they may face their own death. There is no guarantee that they will see out the coming year before God requires their soul of them.

In taking up the call of the biblical text to be sober, Marsden inevitably turned his attention to drunkenness in the colony. He made several appeals to his hearers not to be drunk and spoke of some specific incidents of drunkenness within the colony that led to disaster:

> How many individuals even in this colony have been brought to ruin & destruction by, and also many families have been greatly injured. We have seen persons inflamed by drunkenness to commit adultery, robbery & murder. (Sermon 31:4)

There is nothing peculiar to the colonial experience here which is not uncommon to all societies. People in "drunken fits" are known to be arrested by death in every society and every age. And yet a comment in this sermon relates to the death rate in the colony. Marsden was not only concerned about the high death rate due to drunkenness, but he also stated that the death rate was higher in infancy and "the bloom of life" than those who reach old age:

> We see more cut off either in their infancy, or in the bloom of age life, than what come to the grave in old age. (Sermon 31:16-17)

While in this sermon Marsden expressed concern about high infant mortality, rates in the colony were no different to those in England. Milton Lewis reports that, "Infant death rates in large colonial cities were often of much the same order as those reported in English cities".[80] Marsden may have had in mind that many of those who died in the streets from drunkenness were in the "bloom of life". Burn was probably about 40 when he died at the hand of the butcher. Drunkenness remained a continual problem for the colony both within and outside the prisons. A parliamentary committee of inquiry in 1849 into the administration of Darlinghurst gaol found, "debauchery, drunkenness and irregularity of every kind".[81]

## Sabbath neglect, Gambling and other sins

Compulsory church attendance for soldiers and convicts alike in the early colony was the initial, but never enforced, expectation. As an

---

80 Milton James Lewis, *The People's Health: Public Health in Australia, 1788–1950*. Westport: Greenwood Publishing Group, 2003. p.59.
81 'COUNCIL PAPER.' *The Argus*. Melbourne, Vic. 1848 – 1957. 1 Sep 1849. p. 4. http://nla.gov.au/nla.news-article4765015 Accessed. 22 Dec 2013

example, on Christmas Day 1793 in Johnson's newly-constructed church building, designed to hold 500 people, there were just forty or so in attendance. Marsden found that church attendance did not improve until a much later time. In his preaching he expressed concern that many in the colony did not attend church. There are those:

> who never upon any occasion enter the house of God. Many I know whom I have never seen at a place of public worship upon any occasion. (58:17-18)

But it also seems Marsden did not hold much confidence that those who did attend would gain much benefit. There were many who attended church, "but never regard one word they hear" (Sermon 58:18). However, in his more compassionate moments Marsden was able to hold out, to those who might hear something of his preaching, a word of grace:

> None need to fear to come, who wish to know the Lord however sinful they may be. The precious blood of Jesus is sufficient to atone for all sins. (Sermon 58:24)

Of important note is what Marsden said about those who had come to the colony as convicts. He believed they may well have had better prospects but because of a spiritual condition had fallen "into the snares of the devil":

> How many hundreds are there in this Colony who at one period of their lives had a fair prospect of happiness and honour and comfort before they fell into the snares of the devil, when their understandings were blinded by sin, their passions enslaved, and their hearts hardened. Such men have gone on

progressively from crime to crime until they have ruined their fortunes, and characters and many have, and forfeighted *(sic)* their live *(sic)* or liberty to the State. (Sermon 61:8-9)

It is only the preacher, who has a spiritual perspective on life, who can express such a view of why people have come to a life of crime. At a time when there were more convicts than free settlers in the colony, Marsden noted:

> What an awful scene have the greatest part of this Colony before them. I need not say you are ungodly. I need not tell you that you are sinners. (Sermon 68:11)

Gambling was supposed to be illegal in the colony yet the authorities mostly turned a blind eye to it. Marsden, however, saw that gambling led many into crime:

> Gaming is also a great cause of this sin. Many there are probably in this Colony who would never have openly violated this command, thou shalt not steal, if they had not been addicted to this vice of gaming. (Sermon 75:8)

He said he thought many would agree that the beginning of their troubles could be seen in their involvement in gambling and yet, like his comments on what has led many into crime, he spoke of gambling in terms of its being a spiritual issue:

> I doubt not but there are many in this Colony who may date the beginning of their misfortunes from their love of gaming, & yet notwithstanding all the punishment they have suffered in consequence of (it) even banishment from their country & friends besides many other unknown calamities which they

would never have experienced are yet as fond of this vice as they were the very first day they committed it, and are not yet convinced of its evil tendency. Nothing can demonstrate more strongly how blind we are to our real interest than the general conduct of mankind. No punishments are equal to bring them to reflection nor even the sanctions of the divine law, which are eternal rewards & punishments sufficient to deter them from vice. (Sermon 78:9)

Turning his attention to other crimes, in Sermon 75:11 Marsden says there was no reason for stealing in the colony because there was no real want amongst them. With only a little bit of effort, everyone could be comfortable:

> In every country men have temptations to commit this sin, but perhaps there is no country in the known world where they have so little temptation as in this Colony. There is no real want possibly existing amongst us. Every person may be easy and comfortable in his situation provided he only be (is) industrious. Every person may abound in plenty without extreme labour and toil. It requires no more than a bare moderate industry to live well here.

The establishment of a penal colony at Botany Bay had met with unrelenting ridicule from some quarters at its very suggestion. It was regarded as a "regressive step and an inhumane solution to the nation's penal problems".[82] Despite this attitude back home Marsden believed that the colony provided great opportunity for anyone "with moderate industry to live well". The ensuing prosperity of some

---

82  Smith, *Australia's Birthstain*. p. 203.

emancipists bears testimony to this. And yet Marsden bemoans, "we find that there are hundreds in this Colony who cannot be induced to labour for their own support" (Sermon 75:13). They "choose to starve and steal" rather than to "live by honest industry".

## The general character of the people of the colony

Marsden's disquiet at the general lack of concern in the colony for the lives of those who lay dying of intoxication in the streets has been noted above. In Sermon 86:18 he stated:

> If we were to judge from the general character and conduct of the inhabitants of this Colony, we should be ready to infer that God had in his righteous displeasure given many up to their own heart's lusts.

In another sermon Marsden compared the colonists to the people of ancient Corinth to whom the apostle Paul wrote, condemning their immoral behaviour:

> Tho it is upwards of seventeen hundred years since the great apostle of the gentiles gave this account of the Corinthians, yet had he been sent at the present day he would have to preach the gospel in this Colony, he would have found it necessary to have addressed too many of us in the same language he addressed the heathens in this passage. (88:7)

Marsden saw the sin of fornication as one of the most serious among them:

> The people of Corinth were addicted to the sin of fornication and are not we guilty of this abominable sin as much as the

most ignorant heathens? Perhaps there never was so small a society as we are so much given up to the commission of this sin. (88:19-20)

It is clear that Marsden's understanding was that immorality was rife in the colony. He wondered out loud if it is not true to say that there was not more immorality in the colony than in any other society.

Scattered throughout the sermons there are brief comments on other immoral behaviours that are simply worth noting for Marsden's understanding of behaviour in the colony.

## On sodomy

The Corinthians were also charged with sodomy. And I would to God this sin has no existence amongst us, but this sin is too black and shocking for me to dwell upon here. Only let such persons know that they shall not inherit the kingdom of God. (88:21)

The Select Committee on Transportation in 1837, known as the Molesworth Committee, declared that the system of transportation, which assigned convicts as servants and labourers to free settlers, was nothing more than slavery and also believed transportation was the cause of homosexual activity.[83] Babette Smith makes a cogent case that the report of Molesworth was more to do with the sensitivities of the conservative evangelical clergymen of the

---

83  British Parliamentary Papers. Vol. 19 No. 518. pp. 5-317 and Vol. 22. pp. 1-139.

colony than reality.[84] As noted earlier however, Smith allows her own prejudices to show when she overstates the case with regard to perceptions of the morality of the women convicts when she says that Marsden, "played such a significant role in creating their bad reputation" and quotes Lieutenant Ralph Clark's comments about "damned whores".[85] If, as the quotation from Clark shows, the women had a bad reputation before Marsden had even arrived in the colony, he can hardly be blamed for having a 'significant role in creating their bad reputation" especially by the strange logic that it was his "campaign to reform the morals of the women convicts" that created their bad reputation.

Yet Marsden's comment in Sermon 88 on homosexual activity cannot be discounted. While the comment is not proof to backup Molesworth's assertions it does indicate that homosexual activity was known in the colony. In a letter to Wilberforce in February 1800 Marsden urged his friend to exert his influence to encourage more women into the colony.[86] Yarwood believes this request from Marsden came as a result of his desire not to see young girls, born in the colony from illegitimate liaisons, ending up in prostitution due to an ongoing shortage of women in the colony. Yet it may have also included the thought that with sufficient women available, men may have not been tempted into homosexual activity.

---

84  Smith. *Birthstain*. pp. 200-221. 25 Clergy in Van Diemen's Land had signed a petition in July 1846 sent to the Home Office asking for the end to the probation system in that colony because they believed it encouraged homosexual practices. See Correspondence Relative to Convict Discipline 1847 Vol. 8. p. 44. Cited in *Fatal Shore* p. 531.
85  Smith. *Birthstain*. pp. 206-207
86  Quoted by Yarwood. *Great Survivor*. p.74.

## On reviling

The Corinthians were guilty of reviling one another. Are we free from this sin? Many of us study to slander our neighbour and injure his character and reputation in the world. (88:22)

It is tempting to see an autobiographical note in this statement as Marsden faced many accusations that sought to "injure his character". Already noted is the letter published in the *Sydney Gazette* by *"Philo Free"*. Another letter by *"A Free Settler"*[87] accused Marsden of avarice. Governor Brisbane's view that Marsden was too involved in trade has been noted earlier and is a comment that continues to cause a negative assessment of his character. Over and above all these issues stands Macquarie's dealing with Marsden when their relationship finally broke down irreparably. On 8 January 1818 Marsden was summonsed to appear before the Governor. Macquarie mistakenly believed Marsden to have been the author of a letter to the Home Office complaining of Macquarie's administration. In front of William Cowper, J. T. Campbell and Lieutenant Watts, Macquarie read a prepared statement in which he declared Marsden to be "a secret Enemy of mine" and "the Head of a Seditious Low Cabal". Macquarie then said that he consequently regarded Marsden "unworthy of mixing in Private Society or intercourse with me" and informed him that "I never wish to see you excepting on Public Duty".[88] Cognisant of the Governor's strong opposition to him, Marsden later offered his resignation from his position as Magistrate.[89] Macquarie appears

---

87 This letter is discussed more fully in the following section.
88 Letter from Macquarie to Marsden. 8 January, 1818. III. Correspondence of Lachlan Macquarie, 12 May 1809–16 June 1822. State Library NSW. A 797.
89 Letter from Marsden to Macquarie. 10 March, 1818. *Bigge Appendix*. ML. Box 16. p.2145

to have ignored the letter, but must have taken some delight in causing to be published in the Gazette two weeks later a terse announcement that the Governor was "pleased to dispense with the services of the Rev Samuel Marsden as Justice of the Peace and Magistrate at Parramatta".[90] This must have been particularly galling for Marsden. In January, just days after Macquarie had notified him that he never wished to see him again, the Rev Robert Cartwright had resigned his position as Magistrate. The *Gazette* on that occasion recorded the Governor's high praise of Cartwright and his regret at the loss to the community.[91] Marsden may well have had these events in mind as he prepared Sermon 88. His own character and reputation had been slandered and he could have believed that Macquarie was one of those "many" in the colony who "study to slander" those with whom they disagree.

## On extortion and avarice

> The Corinthians were also guilty of extortion. Are not we also justly chargeable with this crime? I must confess that this extortion is become so common amongst us, that we seem to have forgot that there is such a sin in the world. I believe that extortion was never committed with more agrivating *(sic)* circumstances attending it than what it hath been here. Many seem to think that they may, without extortion, without any injustice to their buier *(sic)*, take any price for the articles they may have for sail *(sic)*, their avarice craves. (88:23)

---

90 *Sydney Gazette.* 28 March, 1818.
91 *Sydney Gazette.* 31 January, 1818.

Numbers of incidents of extortion and avarice could be named as those Marsden might have had in mind in this sermon. From as early as 1803 the *Sydney Gazette* was reporting bakers being brought before the Magistrates and fined for selling short-weight loaves of bread. The *Gazette* reports the practice continuing for decades. One Benjamin Barrow, a recidivist short-weight baker was brought before Magistrate Marsden on 16 October, 1813. Barrow was "charged with exposing for sale 13 loaves short of weight" and was fined three pounds ten shillings.[92]

Another form of extortion can be seen within the colonial military ranks. The military officers at the time of Governor King were enjoying exorbitant profits from the sale of imported spirits. King tried to restrict this trade only to find, through the economic laws of supply and demand, the cost to the public increased. Marsden himself was caught up in an apparent extortion racket when grain growers were holding onto their crops for a better price while government stores were empty.

The farmers of the colony were not exempt from accusations of extortion. The *Gazette* of 5 February, 1814 reported the Governor's Order to growers of grain that if they did not sell their grain at a reasonable price to the stores he would be forced to bypass them and buy imported grain which could "be done at half the Price now paid for that purchased in this Colony". This extortion of government was particularly obnoxious said the Governor because these farmers stood, "considerably indebted to the Crown" for cattle, land and government men. He further declared that this order was to be read by the chaplains over two Sunday mornings. While Marsden may have been one of the recalcitrant grain growers, he condescended

92  *Sydney Gazette*. 23 October, 1813

to read the Order on the first Sunday but refused to do so again on the second. The Governor's ire was raised, letters were sent backwards and forwards to London and Marsden found himself at odds with Macquarie again after some quiet years since his refusal to be a Commissioner of the turn pike road to the Hawkesbury in 1810. Just one month later Marsden found himself in an embarrassing situation. With the appearance in the *Gazette* of several letters from *"A Free Settler"* beginning on 5 March 1814, Marsden was accused of greed in keeping for himself a substantial library of donated books meant for distribution to members of the colony. In a plea to Macquarie to cause the unveiling of the identity of *"A Free Settler"* Marsden denied he had held onto the books because of avarice, but that it was more to do with his general busyness. He just hadn't gotten around to it.[93]

Considering some of these incidents of extortion and avarice in the colony where the finger could well have pointed directly at Marsden, it is interesting to note his comments in this sermon against such practices. Could he have been so bold in his sermon as to simply and blatantly say, "It's not me doing these things!"? Could it be that he just had no concept of his own wrong doing? Or could it be that the accusations against him were overstated? One's own prejudices usually determine the answers to such questions. It is hard to impute motive for good or ill without prejudice. The evidence seems to be against Marsden when it comes to his dealings with the donated books for the lending library. In other dealings the negative accusations seem to come more from those who are predisposed against Marsden. If he was in any sense aware of false dealings in his own business interests it is certainly a very bold statement against such practices in Sermon 88:23.

---

93  9 April, 1814. *Bigge Appendix*. ML. CY1298-9.

## Covetousness

In speaking of the act of Jezebel having Naboth stoned to death and Ahab subsequently taking all his property, Marsden speaks against the sin of covetousness:

> Dreadful as this was, and far surpassing what is commonly found in the British nation, it is in many respects imitated by many amongst us. It is surely no uncommon thing for men at this day to covet what does not belong to them and so inordinately to desire it as to use unlawful (& dishonest) means of obtaining it. (91:7)

Here Marsden is following Simeon, but whereas Simeon speaks in general terms Marsden is specific in applying the teaching to "many amongst us".

## On the receiving of stolen goods

> Let valuable articles be offered for sale, tho the possessor has obtained them by dishonest means, how few will turn them away. If they can only protect themselves from the lap of the law, they give themselves no further concern, but will connive at the (conduct of) [the] common (thief) and suborn to conceal his thefts if they can only gain anything by so doing. Alas the world is full of characters whose hearts are set on covetous practices, and when they are likely to be detected and brought to justice will deliberately perjure themselves on all occasions with the utmost unconcern, as if this was no crime. If we presume to remonstrate with such persons we shall soon see how indignantly they take

reproof tho conscious of their guilt. They labour to substitute impudence & assurance for innocence and integrity. (91:8-9)

In Sermon 91 Marsden seems to have an autobiographical note, indicating that his own remonstrations with sins in the colony tended to meet with less than godly repentance.

> The conduct of Ahab serves to shew what is in the heart of all wicked men against the faithful ministers of the Lord. They are sent as God's monitors to shew the house of Jacob their sins. But who welcomes them in that character? Let them go to any company or to any individual that is violating the laws of God and let them testify against the evil that is committed. Will their admonitions be received with thankfulness. Will not their interposition be deemed rather an impertinent intrusion? And will not the minister become an object of hatred as Elijah was? Yes, such is the light in which is the light in which his conduct will be viewed, however gross and unjustifiable the sin is that has been committed and reproved men cannot bear to have their favourite sins touched. They immediately shew their enmity and indignation. (91:10-11)

Marsden recognised all the trouble within the colony caused by the many and various crimes he dealt with as a Magistrate. Surprisingly there is another trouble that he observed was not present but wished it was. As only one who had a concern for the spiritual state of the colony and its people, Marsden bemoaned the lack of persecution for righteousness sake within the colony. He wished there were more:

> It is many *(sic)* be remarked that in the Colony there is little persecution for righteousness sake. What is the reason of

> this. Because there is little righteousness among us. There is nothing to excite persecution. I would to God there were. (97:11-12)

The lack of persecution for righteousness sake is indicative of all the unrighteousness Marsden observed. While he listed all the troubles that came upon the members of the colony because of extortion, avarice, reviling, covetousness and the like, he would rather that the only troubles that came were to do with persecution that arises against those who are seeking to live in the world according to God's righteousness.

## On foul language

> The common conversation of many of you is nothing but obscene and impure language. ... You can hardly open your mouths without belohing *(sic)* out oaths, curses & blasphemes. (97:13)

Marsden showed concern for the next generation of the effects of sinful behaviour within the colony:

> You have sold yourselves to work iniquity and will be guilty of as many crimes while you live as God & the society in which you are will allow you, but it is necessary that you should be checked and restrained for the good and wellbeing of the rising generation, lest they should imitate your spirit & manners and follow you in the road to ruin & destruction. (97:15)

## Soil Notes

Included with the collection of Marsden's sermons in Moore College, is a series of notes on soil. While Karskens notes that the image of early farmers in the colony as "hopeless, inept, lazy, sinfully wasteful" came from observations of visitors to the colony,[94] Marsden says much the same thing. In his Soil Notes he bemoans the fact that to date (though the date of this document is not known) government has not sent anyone who knows anything about agriculture to oversee the work of farming.

> Unfortunately for this Colony there never was any professional husbandman sent out by government to this day to superintend the cultivation of the ground and to point out the best mode for carrying on the concerns of agriculture. (Soil Notes:7)

Cultivation had been carried out by those who knew nothing about it, or if there were those with knowledge, they were occupied with other duties:

> The whole of this important science upon (the precepts of) which the riches and poverty of a nation depend has been managed hitherto either by persons who had no knowledge of farming on their arrival in the Colony, or if any officer happened to have know any thing of agriculture he had other concerns to attend to in the line of his profession, which prevented him from giving up his time & attention to these studies. (Soil Notes:7-8)

---

94  Karskens. *The Colony*. p.115.

Marsden also spoke of the inappropriateness of giving the work of cultivation to a criminal class who had known nothing but idleness:

> Experience has already clearly evinced what little advantage the Colony is likely to derive from permitting such persons as have been prisoners to become settlers. These men in general have not been brought up in the habits of industry, but of extreme idleness. They have the greatest aversion to labour, to subordination and good government. Their idle, licentious & ungovernable habits are fixed in many of them for life. They set no value whatever on property. Present gratification is their only object. Their farm, their crops, their stock and all they posses they will sell for the mear sake of indulging themselves in a few bottles of liquor. (Soil Notes:8-9)

A further objection Marsden raised against former convicts being given grants of land in the hope that they might become prosperous farmers was their complete lack of knowledge of the principles of cultivation.

> There is another urgent objection against many of the prisoners becoming settlers when the time of their servitude expires, which is their total ignorance of agriculture. When they have obtained a grant of land they are at a loss how to proceed to its cultivation. Many of them have been known to sow their lands with wheat without so much as previously breaking up the ground, it being in its original state, not so much as an hoe or spade put into it. After the wheat is sown they have just chopped the ground over two or three inches deep and left it to take its chance. This method they have adopted partly thro ignorance & partly thro idleness. (Soil Notes:9-10)

In Soil Notes:11 Marsden noted one further problem:

> If there happens in a district to be a labourious (sic) industrious man ~~in a district~~ who is anxious to obtain a competence (for himself and family) and to live comfortably he is sure to be plundered of his grain & stock ~~constantly~~ by his idle licentious neighbours. This is a dreadful evil and puts the severest check upon the industry even of the well disposed. A man and his family may labour but they are never certain of enjoying the fruits of it. If they posses anything they run a risque not only of losing their property but their lives if they dare to defend it.

Plundering and risk to life await the industrious farmer and in Marsden's estimation:

> At present there can be no comparison between the number of the ~~idle~~ ignorant idle & profligate (land holders) ~~settlers~~ and the experienced industrious & sober, who have been allowed to become settlers. The number of the former so far exceeds the latter.

As Karskens has made us aware, visitors to the colony made many of the same observations as Marsden has done in these notes on soil and the men who farm it. The visitors and Marsden were not alone in these observations. Governor Macquarie was also so disturbed by what he saw in the Nepean and Hawkesbury districts on his inspection tour following the general muster that he was moved to write a decree on 9 December 1815 to encourage better farming practices. He noted that "among the lower Order of the Settlers great Slovenliness and neglect of the most obvious and necessary Duties of Farmers were but too frequent and evident in their personal Appearance, and the State of their Farms, in Regard to Cultivation and Improvement". He further observed that the "Farms, although long in a certain Degree of Cultivation, still remained totally devoid of Fences, whereby the Crops of Grain are continually exposed to the Inroads of wandering Herds and Flocks, and are frequently thereby destroyed".[95]

The slovenly appearance of the farmers and their farms disturbed Macquarie. In the same decree he encouraged them not to neglect the Sabbath and called them to a pious observance of the day. It is interesting to note that Macquarie and Marsden are in full agreement on these issues. It is a great pity that a power struggle between them prevented them from working together for what, in some ways, were the same goals.

## Christian Charity

Most of the references in Marsden's preaching that refer to events or conduct in the colony we have looked at so far have been moral issues which he addressed in the hope of exciting some spiritual reform. A significant reference to another event in the colony excited Marsden's call on his people to exhibit Christian charity to those in need. The wreck of the *Edward Lombe*, Sydney's first ship wreck gave Marsden the opportunity to call upon his congregation to show Christian charity to those left destitute by the wreck. He encouraged them to give generously out of Christian duty and for the eternal reward they will receive.

---

95  *Sydney Gazette*. Saturday, 16 December, 1815.

## Conclusion

The Rev Samuel Marsden was a man of extraordinary energy and foresight. Even his nemesis, Governor Lachlan Macquarie, wrote that in his busyness Marsden's "deportment is at all times that of a person the most gay and happy; ... he was by far the most cheerful person I met in the Colony". All this despite the fact that he had "his hands full of work".[96]

While he involved himself fully in the commercial, judicial and political interests of the colony he remained faithful to his own desire to preach the everlasting gospel and to the desires of those who sent him to New South Wales, that he would take the gospel to the people of the South Seas.

As a preacher, Marsden's sermons show that he was a man of compassion and pastoral empathy, a man who had a clear appreciation of the roles of magistrates, governors and clergy, a man who had a strong understanding of how he believed God had ordered society.

He had large numbers of people listening to his message Sunday by Sunday. An account by a member of the "Society of Friends", James Backhouse, as he travelled through NSW with George Washington Walker in 1835 notes that, "The Episcopal congregation, at Parramatta, is attended by from 500 to 600 persons" on Sunday mornings.[97] Governor King wrote that church services at St. John's Parramatta were, "very numerously attended".[98]

Marsden was a visionary when it came to strategizing for

---

96 Lachlan Macquarie. *A Letter to the Right Honourable Viscount Sidmouth.* London, Rees. 1821 p. 18.
97 George Mackaness, *Fourteen Journeys over the Blue Mountains of New South Wales, 1813–1841.* Horwitz-Grahame. 1965. p. 198.
98 *HRNSW* vol.5 p.324

mission. He saw how missionary efforts in Africa and Malta could spread the good news across the whole African continent and planned for nine years to take the gospel to the people of New Zealand. He was, however, also blinkered in his mission strategy. He was not able to think how to reach the local Aboriginal people who did not respond to his well-tried strategies.

Marsden had a vision for a well ordered society in New South Wales and sought, through his role as magistrate, to have some influence in this area. He was blinkered, however, to the damage his reputation as a harsh magistrate did to his reputation as a minister of the gospel.

Marsden was a man of compassion and vision and yet at times that vision was blinkered. The circumstances in which he preached the gospel in the colony of New South Wales were complex. Within that complexity Marsden made mistakes. At the same time he achieved great things as a preacher, pastor, magistrate and missionary.

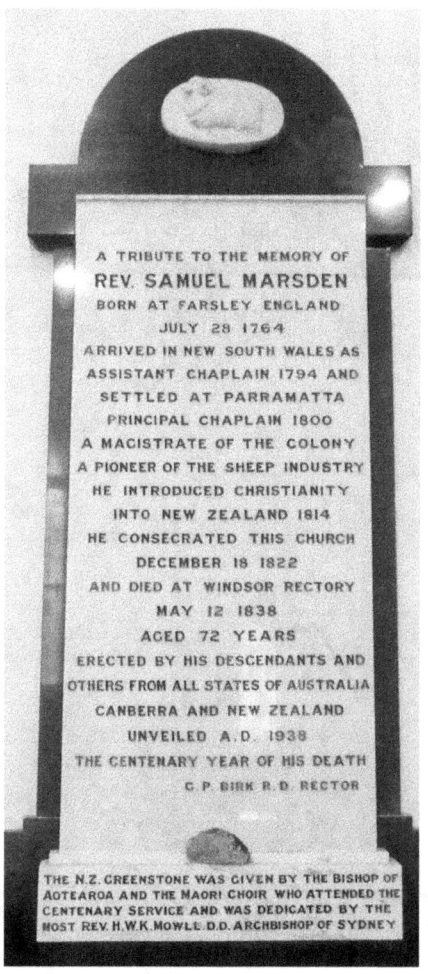

This memorial to Samuel Marsden in the Anglican Church at Windsor NSW shows the confusion around Marsden's date of birth. The memorial says that Marsden was born on 28 July 1764 and that he died on 12 May 1838 aged 72. Simple arithmetic tells us that if Marsden was born on the date indicated he would have actually died at the age of 73. Marsden was in fact born on 26 June 1765.

© Chris Jones.

This font in St John's church Parramatta was the gift of New Zealand craftsmen in 1964 to commemorate Marsden becoming the first person to preach the gospel in New Zealand on Christmas Day, 1814.

© David Pettett

Marsden's communion set.
© David Pettett

# SELECT BIBLIOGRAPHY

Belich, James. *Making Peoples: A History of the New Zealanders from Polynesian Settlement to the End of the Nineteenth Century.* Auckland: Penguin, 1996.

Castle, Tim. "Constructing Death: Newspaper Reports of Executions in Colonial New South Wales, 1826–1837", *Journal of Australian Colonial History* 9, no. 2. 2007.

Castle, "Watching Them Hang. Capital Punishment and Public Support in Colonial New South Wales, 1826–1836", *History Australia* 5, no. 2. 2008.

Davidson, Allan; Lange, Stuart; Lineham, Peter; Puckey, Adrienne (Eds) *Te Rongopai 1814 'Takoto te pai!' Bicentenary reflections on Christian beginnings and developments in Aotearoa New Zealand.* General Synod Office. Auckland. 2014.

Ellis, M. H. *Lachlan Macquarie.* Sydney: Angus & Robertson. 1952.

Falloon, Malcolm. "'Openings of Providence": The shaping of Marsden's missionary vision for New Zealand.' In Peter G. Bolt & David B. Pettett Eds. *Launching Marsden's Mission; The Beginnings of the Church Missionary Society in New Zealand, viewed from New South Wales.* London. Latimer Press. 2014.

Hughes, Robert. *The Fatal Shore: A History of Transportation of Convicts to Australia, 1787–1868.* London, The Havill Press. 1987

Jones, Alison and Jenkins, Kuni. *Words between Us – He Korero First Maori – Pakeha Conversations on Paper.* Wellington. Huia Publishers. 2011.

Karskens, Grace. *The Colony: A History of Early Sydney.* Sydney. Allen & Unwin. 2009.

Lake, Meredith. "Samuel Marsden, Work and the Limits of Evangelical Humanitarianism", *History Australia* Vol 7, no. 3 (2010).

Lewis, Milton James. *The People's Health: Public Health in Australia, 1788–1950*. Westport: Greenwood Publishing Group, 2003.

Mackaness, George. (Ed.) *Fourteen Journeys over the Blue Mountains of New South Wales, 1813–1841*. Horwitz-Grahame. 1965.

Mackaness, George. (Ed.) *Some Private Correspondence of the Rev Samuel Marsden and Family 1794–1824*. Sydney. Mackaness. 1942.

Marsden, John Buxton and Drummond, James. *Life and Work of Samuel Marsden*. London: Whitcombe and Tombs Limited, 1913.

Quinn, Richard. *Samuel Marsden: Altar Ego*. Wellington. Dunmore Publishing Ltd. 2008.

Roberts, M. J. D. *Making English morals: voluntary association and moral reform in England, 1787–1886*. Cambridge. Cambridge University Press. 2004.

Salt, Annette. *These Outcast Women: The Parramatta Female Factory 1821–1848*. Macquarie Colonial Papers. Sydney. Hale & Iremonger. 1984.

Smith, Babette. *Australia's Birthstain: The Startling Legacy of the Convict Era*. Crows Nest, N.S.W. Allen & Unwin. 2008.

Standfield, Rachel. *Race and Identity in the Tasman World, 1769–1840*. London. Pickering & Chatto. 2012.

Woods, G. D. "A History of Criminal Law in New South Wales the Colonial Period, 1788–1900", ed. Mark Findlay Chris Cunneen, Julie Stubbs, *Sydney Institute of Criminology Monograph Series No 17*. Sydney: The Federation Press, 2002

Yarwood, A. T. *Marsden of Parramatta*. Kenthurst, N.S.W.: Kangaroo Press, 1986.

Yarwood, A. T. 'Marsden, Samuel (1765–1838)', *Australian Dictionary of Biography*. Volume 2. Melbourne University Press. 1967. pp 207–212.

Yarwood, A. T. *Samuel Marsden: The Great Survivor*. Carlton, Vic. Melbourne University Press. 1977.

**Cover picture: 'Samuel Marsden preaching at Oihi Bay, Christmas 1814' by Kenneth Watkins.**
John Kinder Theological Library. Archives reference: KIN 68/1/9

**Title page picture: Rev Samuel Marsden by James Fittler. Engraving.**
Hocken Collections, Uare Taoka o Hakena, University of Otago

# ABOUT THE AUTHOR

OVER THE PAST 38 YEARS David Pettett has been in Christian ministry in several Sydney parishes. He has been a missionary, church planting in Japan, and a chaplain in the Royal Australian Navy, in hospitals and prisons. He has been the Head Chaplain in the Anglican Diocese of Sydney managing chaplains in prisons, hospitals, mental health, juvenile justice and aged care. David graduated from Moore Theological College, Sydney in 1978, has a Th. L. and Th. Schol. from the Australian College of Theology, a Masters in Pastoral Care and Counselling from the Sydney College of Divinity, a Graduate Certificate in Pastoral Supervision from St. Mark's, Canberra, and a Ph. D. in history from Macquarie University. David's Ph. D. focused on the sermons of Samuel Marsden. He is currently working on a critical edition of Marsden's sermons.

www.ingramcontent.com/pod-product-compliance
Lightning Source LLC
Chambersburg PA
CBHW050541300426
44113CB00012B/2211